Small Boat Down The Years is the twentieth and last of Roger Pilkington's acclaimed and successful *Small Boat* series, which charted over forty years of travel and exploration on the inland waterways of England and Europe.

Here, the author looks back over some of the most remarkable and memorable events which befell him and his travelling companions during the many journeys he undertook. From the Fenlands surrounding Cambridge to early voyages on the Thames, from the waterways of Belgium and Holland to the great Göta river in Sweden, no journey was without incident, and Roger Pilkington's natural humour and humanity ensure that they come brilliantly alive in the telling.

Thus does a moving boat cause insurmountable problems for a policeman trying to carry out H M Government's national census on the Thames, the author's first boat *Commodore* manage to negotiate a bridge three feet too low, and his second boat *Thames Commodore* and its crew achieve the removal of an offending bridge and the restoration of an old canal in Sweden.

Like all the other *Small Boat* books, *Small Boat Down the Years* combines boating with science, engineering, history and legend, and gives practical and useful advice for navigating some of the world's most famous canals and rivers – and many of its least. As a delightful summation of *Commodore's* and *Thames Commodore's* journeys down the years, it is a must for the active inland voyager, and any of the thousands of *Small Boat* armchair fans around the world.

Roger Pilkington has had more than fifty books published including the twenty in the best-selling *Small Boat* series, whose voyages then inspired a series of children's adventure books, one of which was featured on the BBC's *Jackanory*. A regular contributor to the *Sunday Telegraph*, he and his wife divide their time between homes in Jersey and Montouliers in France. The establishment of his second home on French soil is the subject of the successful *One Foot in France*, also available as a Temple House paperback.

Small Boat Down The Years

Roger Pilkington

Temple House Books
Sussex, England

Temple House Books
is an imprint of
The Book Guild Ltd.

The Book Guild Ltd.
25 High Street,
Lewes, Sussex

First published 1987 by J. M. Pearson & Son (Publishers) Ltd.
© Roger Pilkington 1987

This edition published 1994

Typesetting by Character Graphics, Taunton, Somerset

Printed in Great Britain by
Antony Rowe Ltd.
Chippenham, Wiltshire

A catalogue record for this book is
available from the British Library

ISBN 0 86332 944 6

Contents

I

Early Rivers

T his book is about rivers and canals. It is in no way a guide to waterway networks, and I very much doubt if any would-be navigator will find it of help when crossing Europe in his own boat, except perhaps as relaxation when he is held up for a day or two because the gate of the lock ahead has come off its hinges. Nor is it intended to be autobiographical. I had the good fortune to become infected with a love of inland waterways at a time when their delights were known only to the very few who used them for their own pleasure and who were not engaged in carrying coal from pit to power station, or floating rafts of timber down the streams of the far north.

My enthusiasm for waterways was developed, not inherited. I had no navigators, inland or otherwise, among my ancestors and, even if one of England's earliest artificial channels ended at the town where I was born and brought up, the only times I ever glimpsed the St Helens Canal was when crossing it in the outskirts of Warrington. Just occasionally the road traffic would be halted because the bridge which crossed the canal almost at water level had been swung away to let a tired old horse haul doggedly through the gap a dirty lighter piled with coal and steered by an individual whose clothing and face were as black as those of the man who came to sweep our chimneys. The family chauffeur frowned, regarding the existence of the canal as an annoying hindrance to his driving. But for myself the sight held something of wonder, and if on the same journey we were again held up at the much mightier swing-bridge on the further side of the town where the road crossed the Manchester Ship Canal, then for myself the event was one of delight. I would jump out of the car and stand at the barrier to watch as a mighty cargo steamer was hauled slowly through the gap by its attendant tugs. And each of these swinging bridges carried the implicit message that dozens of cars and lorries, however urgent their business, took second place to a ship, whether tall-funnelled cargo-liner or a grubby coal lighter behind its arthritic horse.

Very soon my awareness of canals was extended by my going to school
at Rugby, where the towpath of the Oxford Canal provided one of the
more pleasant of the Sunday walks. Horse-drawn boats would come gliding
silently round the hill at Newbold to disappear mysteriously into the cavern
mouth of the short tunnel. And sometimes the vault would echo with the
heavy pop-pop-pop of a more modern craft, an oil-engined narrowboat
registered in Coventry with lace-work china plates hung inside the doorway,
or perhaps a Samuel Barlow boat with its romantic castles painted on the
panels and the cabin sides in bright red and green, and with the proprietor's
name impeccably painted in shaded seriffed lettering. It was another twenty
years before I went on that canal in a boat, but from school I explored it
for many miles on skates when it lay frozen stiff in the grip of hard winters,
and in summertime I more than once rode over on my bicycle to Braunston
and had a view of the narrowboats ranged along the cut and in the basins,
the blue smoke from their brass-ringed chimneys drifting easily along the
path and over the hedgerows and the surly dogs keeping a watchful eye
on each other from the cabin tops.

Later, at the university of Freiburg, I had the chance when we cycled
out on laboratory excursions to see the Rhine in all its grandeur where it
flowed past the cathedral hill of Breisach as a swift, grey, swirling stream.
It was crossed there by a bridge of boats, a row of large pontoons anchored
in the current and carrying a rumbling roadway of planks. A pair of these
craft could be uncoupled in the centre of the river and hauled out of the
gap to allow a tow-train to pass on its way upstream to Basle in Switzerland,
but so great was the current in springtime that the bridge might have to
stay open for hours at a time. On one occasion we saw the bridge opened
ahead of the powerful tug with its huge smoke-stacks belching and the
mighty paddle-wheels threshing the water, and after we had eaten our
lunch and investigated the insects indigenous to the Eckhartsberg, the last
of the long string of lighters was not yet clear of the gap. It was an
awe-inspiring, powerful sight, that great river, and I never dreamed that
thirty years later I would myself be steering up it. By then its current had
gone and a high bridge replaced the ancient bridge of boats to the Alsatian
shore, but it had lost none of the splendour of its mighty traffic, nor its
romance as a highway of trade for nearly two thousand years.

My first aquatic command was at Cambridge. It was unthinkable to
reside on the edge of a navigable river and have no chance to explore it,
so in the first summer of my research days my wife and I ventured
downstream aboard one of the cruisers that could be hired from Banham's
Yard at Chesterton. Soon we came to know intimately the rivers of the
strange, flattish Fenland, penetrating any creek or lode where there was
water enough and pursuing it to the limit of navigability. They were not
spectacular, these streams of the fens, but they were the haunts of reed

warblers and buntings and it was there that for the first time i saw snipe rising in spiral flight then diving down with the tail feathers protruded to produce that extraordinary sound, half mechanical and half goat-like, known to bird-lovers as 'drumming'. Once I caught a glimpse of a bittern where it stood motionless in the reeds, its bill pointed upward as it tried to pretend that it was only the base of a clump of sedge.

These early voyages up the deserted rivers of the Fenland, where civilisation appeared only rarely in the form of a bridge or a distant church tower, taught me enough about handling a motor-vessel for me at least to summon up sufficient courage to undertake the trip of exploration I wanted more than any other, which was to penetrate the Middle Level. This involved following the Ouse between its high and somewhat uninteresting banks all the way to Denver Sluice, where a massive erection of floodgates kept out the rising water of the tidal estuary. As is usual at such places, one had to wait until the levels were right, before the gates could be wound high overhead, and the passage was clear. When this happened there could be no turning back, and it was with some misgivings that I took the boat out in wind and rain into the soupy, silty water which seemed to me to be moving too fast. I had never before been in a tideway, and although I only had to steer Banham's *Crusader* down it for less than a quarter of a mile before turning out of it again on the further side and passing through Salter's Lode Lock, I felt heroic if not precisely intrepid. It was a tidal run that was all over in little more than a minute, but one had to begin somewhere.

It was possible in those days, with a certain amount of determination, to enter Well Creek at Salter's Lode and pass by such curious waterways as Popham's Eau, Bevill's Leam, the Old River Nene and King's Dike to reach the Nene at Peterborough. At least, that was the theory; but as one of the locks in that deserted countryside proved to be out of action we never reached the Nene. Not that it mattered, for we had plenty of other things to interest us.

For the sake of variety I decided to return down the old course of the Nene in the dark. It was nearly midnight when we cast off, and the half moon cast a cold, greenish light upon the water. To either side the hoar-frost sparkled on the high banks above the sedge. A dark form appeared, swimming swiftly out of the reeds on the right, crossing ahead of our bow-wave, too large for a water-vole, too lithe for a coypu, of which there were a number in the wild fenland of Cambridgeshire. It was the first otter I had ever seen and, although on the next day I saw another, it was almost the last. In those years the water was savoury if not clear, the fish had not yet been poisoned by the wash-off of fertilisers, swans were not dying in any noticeable number from the ingested lead shot and hooks of careless anglers. The countryside smelled of earth and farmyard manure, not of tractors and superphosphate. England, even in the flatness of its fen country and on a chilly night in April, was at peace with itself, lying silent as if in a dream of content.

None can pretend that the scenery of the Middle Level is the finest in Britain, and yet the fenland waterways have a romance of their own. The wide sky reaching down to the treeless horizon, the thick grey clouds puffed up with pride, the endless expanse of sugar-beet, the forgotten farms tilted back on their heels by the shrinkage of the land, and in April the wide fields striped in red and orange, yellow and white as the tulips burst into bloom; these are glories unknown to those who find their pleasure only in the mountains. Only here and there does the humblest hillock advertise that once there were low islands in the marsh that existed before Cornelius Vermuyden was called from the Netherlands to design the defences against flooding.

I had decided that on reaching Salter's Lode and issuing into the Ouse tideway once more I would not re-enter the river at Denver Sluice but carry the tide right up the twenty miles of the New Bedford river. For ever since one dark and rainy night two years earlier I had wanted to return to that remarkable area traversed by the great channels cut by the eminent engineer to whom Cambridgeshire owes much of its richest land.

Cornelius Vermuyden and his workmen left many a memory behind them. Cottages with Dutch gables, street names such as Le Munterstraate in the little abbey town of Ramsey, the fen drain known as Vermuyden's Eau, and if I remember correctly there is a cottage in Fen Drayton with the inscription *Niet zonder arbeid* over the doorway – Nothing without labour. Originally called in by Charles the First, he tinkered about with the maze of fenland drains and channels, without any very definite plan, and when his banks and sluices failed to keep dry the surrounding land there was delight among the fen-dwellers themselves, who lived by fishing and fowling and had no desire to have their marshland turned into agricultural land. Later he was engaged once more, this time by the Duke of Bedford and a band of investors, and he set about short-circuiting the meandering forty miles of the Ouse above Downham Market with a straight cut. For a while this was successful and a good quantity of land was reclaimed for agriculture, but before long the works collapsed, the sponsors lost their money, and the Duke of Bedford's only reward was to be immortalised in the name of Vermuyden's by-pass waterway which was to become known as the Old Bedford River.

The King now returned to the task, hoping by draining the fens to acquire land which would yield the money of which he was always in need, but Cromwell and Parliament succeeded in stopping the works and closing that possible source of revenue. Now it was the turn of the next Duke of Bedford, who hoped to recoup the losses his father had sustained. Vermuyden must by this time have been more familiar than any other engineer with the problems of the fens and when he was yet again called in to undertake the task of draining them his efforts were crowned with success, although like so many water engineers after him he died in poverty. His scheme was essentially simple. He cut a second bow-string across the forty-mile loop of the Ouse and constructed an area called 'the Washes' – not to be confused with the nearby sea area of the Wash. His bow-string was now double, the Old Bedford River receiving the water from the fens to its side, and evacuating them into the estuary through a sluice, whilst the parallel New Bedford River was tidal without obstruction all the way from Earith to the sea. Each river had a very high outer bank and a lower inner one, so that in times of river floods further inland, or storm-driven surges out at sea, the surplus water could flood over and fill the twenty-mile long reservoir of the Washes between the two, draining off later when the tide had fallen away. Other modifications to the flow of the Ouse have been necessary since Vermuyden's day, because the land has shrunk through pumping and at the same time the sea level has risen, but it was he whose grand scheme converted the area from marsh to fine fertile land.

I have given this all too potted account of the great project of draining the fens of Cambridgeshire and the Isle of Ely because they resulted in the formation of a part of England which is little known outside the area and which always had a strange fascination for me from the day – or rather the night – on which I first discovered it. That was in February of 1937, when I was enmeshed in studies for part two of the Zoology Tripos. It was a wet February, a real February Filldyke, and the dykes of the fenland were filled beyond capacity. Inexorably the Cam crept up the lawns of Kings and Trinity, Magdalene's Benson Court had water almost to the steps of the staircases and, if after taking a bath in the basement one pulled out the plug, there was a chance that muddy water from overloaded street drains would surge in. The banks of the 'lodes' further downstream were hard-pressed and so were those of the Ouse and the two Bedfords, for the only way in which any locality could save its own area from inundation was by turning up the steam on their own lode-pumps to void the water into rivers already overflowing. The first hint that things were getting beyond control came with the news that the Soham lode was breached, the bank had slid, and a string of maintenance barges had gone through the hole into a field of sugar-beet which now lay a fathom or two under water.

It was then that the River Great Ouse Catchment Board appealed for help. Everything was done to try to induce local pump-houses to slacken their delivery, but floods in the Midlands were pouring down through Bedford and St. Neots, Huntingdon and St. Ives. The weirs were level, the torrents raged, the Washes were full to the brim and gales were holding

up the high level of spring tides, preventing the water from running out
to sea. The only possibility that remained was to heighten the outer bank
along the Old Bedford, which was somewhat lower than that of the New
Bedford and so was more liable to flow over. This meant digging, not
with machinery but with spades. Sacks had to be filled with soil from the
fields, dragged up to the bank top and laid along it in a wall, which in
places was two or three bags high.

A party of us from Part Two Zoology volunteered. A bus picked us up
after our respective dinners in Hall, and we set off into the utter blackness
of the unknown. To reach our destination was not easy, for many of the
roads were under water, but I read some names in the light of the bus
headlamps. Strange names they were too, of which I had never heard:
Mepal, Sixteen Foot Drain, Manea, Purls Bridge, Welches Dam. To either
side of the roadway there was nothing to be seen but water, except where
a hamlet stood on very slightly higher ground.

At Welches Dam we got out and were given our spades and bundles of
sacks. Our job was to contain the flood as best we could on the section
of the bank from Welches Dam, where the Forty Foot Drain was pumping
its surplus contents through the bank, to Welney – about five miles down
the bank. We were not alone. There were labourers from the Catchment
Board, County Council men, farmers and their hands, all enthusiastic
hard-working men who dug and heaved in the pouring rain even if they
had not slept for a day and a night. There was no talk in those days of
double overtime, or refusing to work with unpaid volunteers, or consulting
the union about how many sacks one might fill in an hour, or how long
the tea-break would be. It was a determined, exhausted, cheerful, energetic
and happy band of men who slogged away in the downpour. It was England
at its best, England as in those days it so often was.

We were warned by a foreman that if anyone felt the bank move he was
to shout, and we were to drop everything and run back along the top. For
if it had moved it would have let go a tremendous force of water. Just
below where I was working there was a farmhouse with a light in the
upper window, and that window was considerably below the level of my
feet. The ridge of the roof stood lower than the bank top against which
the water was lapping. One of the men working along with me, laying the
sacks of squelching mud as I carried them up on my back and dumped
them, was the farmer himself. He was a somewhat silent man with greying
hair. I asked him whether he though the bank would hold.

"Ay," he said. "She'll hold if it's God's will. An' if it ain't his will,
neither you nor me can make it hold."

"And your house?"

"If the bank slides, the house will go too. There's the wife and two
little ones asleep down there. I don't think it's the will of God to take

them just now. So I reckon the bank should hold. That is, if we keeps at it."

Even in those days his simple, straightforward theology was one that appealed to me. Trust God and do your job, and all would be well – probably. But there might be things the Almighty could not prevent, limits, as it were, to soul-less almightiness.

Oddly enough, there was no means of co-ordinating the output of the pumps which emptied the drains and lodes. They were not on the telephone. So the Catchment Board had set up a headquarters somewhere, to which reports on water levels and the state of the banks could be phoned by villagers, or by inspectors and foremen using the few call-boxes that were to be found in that desolate countryside. A master mind then decided that this weir should be open more, or that pump shut down, so that a united front could be held until the tide sweeping through distant King's Lynn was falling back. The detailed orders of this strategy were phoned to the BBC, which interrupted its broadcasts very much as it does for "Attention all shipping" gale warnings. Thus Beethoven's Violin Concerto might fade away and be replaced by a voice exhorting a pump on the Old West or Popham's Eau to reduce to so many cubic feet per minute. It was all very strange and exciting for those throughout Britain who had little idea where these places might be and did not immediately recognize in the five-hundred-year old drainage waterway known as Morton's Leam the name of a celebrated Archbishop who, though better known for his two-pronged fork of ecclesiastical taxation, was also a man who tried to drain the levels east of Peterborough.

It was sometime around midnight that we were invited to take a quick break for a cup of tea in the Forty Foot pump-house nearby. I trudged through the mud with Mark Pryor, later senior tutor of Trinity, and others of our zoologist gang. It was warm in the pump-house and the machine was chuffing away with long, considered strokes, the beautifully polished valves and the smooth steel of the piston rod gleaming in the light of an oil lamp. It was a welcome break, and perhaps for a moment I envied the engineer as he sat there in an old wicker-chair, savoury smoke drifting from the bowl of his pipe. He sat comfortably in his shirt sleeves, his feet on a small table on which stood a wireless. (Nobody talked about 'radio' in those days.)

Some Palm-Courtish music was trickling from the set to indicate that the transmission was still alive even at that hour. Then it faded, and a polished announcer's voice declared that it had a bulletin from the Catchment Board. There was heavy flooding in the Bedford area it seemed (Bedford town, not the Bedford Level, which was already more or less waterlogged). The weirs at St Neots and various other places on the river were to be kept open to capacity, but to allow a quicker run-off less water was to be voided into the Old Bedford River – which I must again explain is nowhere near Bedford town, with which it only shared a historical duke. "Welches Dam Engine", the voice went on, "reduce to half capacity".

We suddenly felt important as we stood there gratefully sipping mugs of tea from the engineer's enamel jug. We were on the map, on the air, known to the mighty, paternalistic, all-caring and efficient broadcasting authority. We sensed something like a holy respect for the wonder of wireless. At least I did, and I think the others did too. Except the engineer. He leaned forward and flicked off the set.

"Bedford! Who do they think they are? They can keep their own blinking floods. We're not taking them down here, not while I'm running the old pump." He got out of his chair, examined the steam pressure gauge and opened the valve another three or four turns. The gleaming connecting rod began to flash faster, the chuffing of the steam exhaust became more hurried. Satisfied, the engineer resumed his seat. We drank our tea, then trudged out into the damp darkness to resume our work.

When the first light of impending dawn began to tint the sky across the river to the eastward I saw where we were. That is, I found that we were in a position such as I never could have dreamed of. The by-road by which we had come ended at Welches Dam, but I could follow its course toward Manea because it was raised on top of a dyke bank. Beyond it the land lay under water, with here and there the line of a bank, or a pair of forlorn and solitary elms. To the right lay the long line of Vermuyden's Washes, an expanse of water nearly a mile broad and bounded by the outer bank of the New Bedford, disappearing in the limitless distance to curve over the edge of the earth. The line of the horizon could be seen beneath the black stripe of the viaduct two or three miles ahead which carried across the Washes the railway track from Ely to Peterborough. In front of us the only dry land was the narrow top of the bank on which we were working, receding as far as the eye could see as a thin black line amid the water. It was as though we were on an island twenty miles long and a few feet in breadth.

The rain had stopped and the sun edged its way up out of the water, red and ominous. I had a strange feeling of being present at the birth of the world. It was as though the spirit of God moved across the face of the waters and he was calling to the sun "Let there be light" – and there was light.

The scene when I took the *Crusader* up the New Bedford on the rising tide was very different, but just as appealing. Some might consider the run up that long straight line to be dull. Probably there is no stretch of waterway even in Holland which is so straight over a length of two or three hours of navigation, the line ahead cut only by the very matter-of-fact viaduct at Manea and the road bridges at Welney and Mepal, and yet here one is wonderfully conscious of the enormous space and majesty of the sky, falling down to the bluish haze of the slightly raised land further ahead. The Washes, I remember, lay in their temporary guise of summer meadows and fat cows were munching in contemplative fashion among the expanse of buttercups edged with loose-strife. I did not regret that I had chosen that route and little by little my worry at being on tidal water was forgotten.

At the end of the cut the course of the Ouse swung away to the right to Brownshill Staunch – a pleasant name for a lock – and beyond that, past charming villages with their mills built upon the weirs, to Huntingdon. But the route back to Cambridge, completing the circuit of the Isle of Ely, was through the Hermitage Lock into a narrow winding waterway with the nostalgic name of the Old West River, which was the original course of the Ouse before Cornelius Vermuyden changed it.

On the wall of the lockhouse a faded table of tolls was displayed, carefully painted many years before and giving the charges to be levied on cargoes which, however improbable, must once have been expected to pass through the lock. Pigs and sheep, cauldrons of coal, bundles of sedge, chalk, bricks, all had their particular rates, but the only barges that ever came through nowadays were the trains of tubs of the Catchment Board carrying blue gault to staunch the banks, and these were sufficiently rare for a cruiser such as the *Crusader* to be a welcome relief from minding a lock without customers.

I walked up to the cottage where the woman lived who kept the keys and windlasses. There was a stale smell about the place and in her parlour the wallpaper of faded festoons of roses ended raggedly two or three feet above the floor. She noticed that I was looking at it.

"The flood," she said. "That were a night that were. There were such a knockin' about midnight, a thumpin' on the wall and bangin' down below, so my hubby he gets up an' goes down to see who's there. An' afore he gets to the bottom of the stairs he walks right into the water. An' the knockin', you know what it were? The kitchen table goin' round on his own, knockin' on the walls."

It was the water that had taken the wallpaper, and even two years after the event the flood line was clear for all to see.

"The mud were somethin' terrible. We had an inch or two right through the house. Course it ruined the settee and the chairs there. But it might have been worse. The house could have collapsed, an' us asleep in our beds. An' it weren't all bad. You should 'ave seen the big carp as got stuck in the piano."

★   ★   ★

It was in 1947, after moving to Highgate, that I happened one day to be driving home from Guildford and managed to get lost in the maze of roads in outer suburbia. My knowledge of the Thames was hazy and I had not yet discovered that the same placid turgid river which I had often crossed at Southwark or Vauxhall became further upstream a navigation with locks – no less than forty-five as I later discovered – extending all the way to Oxford and beyond. But here was a trim lock with neatly kept flower-beds, white-painted rails and chains to keep people off the tidily clipped grass, and a uniformed keeper in a black waistcoat with brass buttons and the smart white summer cap of the Thames Conservancy. He was leaning against the long, black and white balance beam to swing open one of the gates at the downstream end.

I glanced along the reach below the lock and saw to my astonishment a surprisingly large steamer shaping up for the entrance. She was the *Mapledurham*. She wheezed easily to a halt against the piles. A lad dropped nooses over the bollards and helped to close the gates, then went forward to lend a hand with turning the wheels that raised the paddles. There were fifty or more passengers sitting chatting on the upper deck or leaning over the rails, all of them obviously enjoying their voyage.

The timetable posted on the lockside hut beside the notices of By-laws to be obeyed by those passing "by, through, or over" the locks of the Conservancy showed to my astonishment that there was a regular service of Salter's Steamers between Kingston and Oxford, with two departures daily in either direction. I was amazed, and after watching the steamer depart in the direction of Chertsey I drove home full of excitement. As soon as the summer term of the children's schools was at an end we would take the trip from Kingston.

Even then I had no idea of the sheer loveliness of the Thames and what an exquisite voyage it was to be. There were no cabins on the ship, but the company arranged accommodation at the White Hart at Windsor for the first night and at Shillingford Bridge for the second. There was no catering on board either, but there was ample time for lunch at Henley, and at Abingdon the boat paused for a moment by the bridge so that trays with a splendid hot lunch could be taken on board – for the crew only. And once clear of the London suburbs at Shepperton the river meandered through a countryside that was a water-colour painter's dream, and very, very English. By that I mean that it bore the imprint of centuries of quiet, humble confidence, devoid of any ostentation. It was a shy countryside, but one of unrivalled beauty.

The immediate result of the voyage up to Oxford was to set us wondering why we lived within reach of such a river as the Thames without having a boat upon it. There followed many days of touring boatyards at Boveney and Staines, at Walton and Molesey, Kingston and Teddington to inspect the lists of craft for sale. We went aboard several, but there was always something which was not suitable. Sometimes it was merely the price, but more often it was the size or the lay-out, or the general state of disrepair. We even ranged as far afield as the Ouse and the Cam in our despairing search, and it was our old friends at Banham's who told us of the existence of the Director of Small Craft Disposals, an official who resided in a mansion far out of London and miles from the water, near Wisley Gardens. He was charged with disposing of such surplus units of the Royal Navy as were not in the battleship class, and every few weeks he issued a list of what he had available from the left-overs of their Lordships of the Admiralty.

We started taking the list, only to find that it contained little of interest to us. There might be a tug, lying at some inaccessible place such as Aden. Other craft stationed as close as Lambeth had a way of being concrete fuel pontoons. Some of the ships were too large, others had armour plating and torpedo tubes, and the few ship's lifeboats that came on the market were in bad condition and not worth the trouble of conversion. We also wasted much time and energy in travelling to see craft whose situation was described with the accuracy customary among house agents. One that sounded suitable was "lying at the breakwater" somewhere on the south coast. Full of hope I went down by train, but it proved unnecessary to inspect the vessel in detail. I could see her before the train reached the station. The hull was, as stated "lying at the breakwater" – half on one side of it and half on the other.

Most of the Director's craft were in fact wrecks, but one day an "admiral's barge" came up. The moment I saw her lying off the Gillingham foreshore in the Medway I knew that she was the one for us, and the fact that her huge engines had been taken out meant that a conversion could be planned. I put in a modest offer for the craft and after many weeks had gone by a telegram from Whitehall to Highgate announced that the offer was accepted. Work on conversion was begun at once, the name *Commodore's Barge Hamburg* was shortened to *Commodore*, and just over five months later she dropped down the Medway on the tide to head up the Thames for London. She was a simple but beautiful boat, suitable for the use to which we intended to put her, which was to be a weekender on the Conservancy Thames. I could never in my most irrational dreams have imagined at that time that she was going to range from Uppsala in the north to the Mediterranean in the south, or to be the mother of eighteen books.

It is tempting to sit down and write a book about the Thames, but that has already been done by writers from Samuel Ireland to Sir Alan Herbert. I have even done it twice already myself, and twice is enough. No river in the world is so rich in history – somebody once called the Thames "liquid history" – and if the Rhine has more legends of true love, of chivalry and barbarous murders, the Thames has known dramatic events from the coming of the Romans, who forded it, fortified it at Londinium and sailed upon it, to the Vikings, the Dutch, and the twentieth century Germans, all of whom attacked its shipping and raided the settlements along its shores. For more than a hundred miles the riverside villages and towns have been the homes of artists and writers and poets whose names are known around the world. Matthew Arnold mused along its upper reaches, Samuel Pepys paid a waterman to row him from Old Swan to Putney while he sat in the stern to read Robert Boyle's new work on colours, of which he could understand but little, yet enough to see that Boyle was "a most excellent man". Robert Gibbings canoed upon the river and made his charming woodcuts, Canaletto painted the City reaches as did Kokoschka after him. Famous men who dared to say they believed in times when such outspokenness was dangerous had their heads displayed on pikes at the southern end of London Bridge. Queens were rowed upon the Thames to imprisonment or execution, and just as the Cam flows through one of the world's greatest centres of civilised thought, so too the Thames (or Isis as they like to call it) flows through the other. It is, I think, no accident that Oxford and Cambridge lie on modest rivers. Not fast flowing torrents like the Rhine or Rhône, but gentle streams which in monastic times provided the opportunity for fishing as well as contemplation, and throughout the centuries offered the calm of the flowery meadows with the rooks cawing in the trees, the riverside walks, the lawns and gardens among which intellect could flourish in the morning and evening whilst in the afternoon the muscles could be fortified at the oars of eights, whether fixed pin or swivel.

The Thames was the first river I came to know more intimately than the Cam, and that was thanks to *Commodore*. On our first voyage we entered the Conservancy river at the top of the tideway, passed through Teddington Lock and continued one weekend of early April until we found a home for her which could be her base for several years and was within easy reach of London. This was at Maidenhead, not far below the famous Boulter's Lock, where the iron railings, put to keep the public at such a distance that Edward VII could not hear the comments of the common people about the ladies he took on the river, were scrapped during the last war for their metal, much to the improvement of the lockside.

In the late nineteen-forties the river had not yet become the prey of the entrepreneur. The few boatyards were sleepy places with punts and skiffs as well as a few modest cruisers; camping sites had not been opened up; the discotheque or over-amplified record-player was not invented; the inns had no ambition much beyond roast beef and Yorkshire, and one could stop at a bank or quayside without immediately having to bring out a wallet. Only along the the most popular reaches were there considerable numbers of boats on the move, and even then only at summer week-ends. The river had a grace, a gentle calm which of course has not everywhere vanished, and which perhaps we appreciated particularly because we tended also to use the stream when others did not, in midwinter as well as summer, at midnight as well as by day.

I always considered the Thames even lovelier in winter than summer. Its great woodlands at Cliveden and all the way from above Reading to the Streatley Hills were of beech mixed with such other trees as liked the grey, chalky soil, and they were nearly all deciduous. In summer the dense cloak of green was magnificent, stately, but in the winter months one could see into the woods, glimpsing the contours of the land and sometimes seeing right through the dim mauve net of the meshed branches to another line of gently rolling country beyond. The low sun of a winter morn could penetrate those woodlands, and, reflected from the damp of the trunks and branches, fill them with an unearthly light. Often I wondered whether the earliest inhabitants of the valley saw its loveliness, or whether the denser forest of those days was more likely seen only as a source of food and of fuel for the fires in their simple dwellings. The time to relax and enjoy the beauty of things had not then arrived.

The Streatley Woods first became known to me in my schooldays, when I had constructed a wireless set which took up as much space as fifty or more would today. In the evenings the broadcasting authority, whose taste was impeccable and whose announcers probably still put on dinner jackets to sit before the microphone, had mounted a technical enterprise which in its day was revolutionary. It brought to the listener the plaintive, wandering, trilling and piping song of a nightingale. Somewhere in the Streatley Woods above the Thames crouched the technicians in their earphones watching the flicker of needles on the dials of their apparatus. Nearby an eminent cellist whose name I cannot remember sat on a stool, the spike of her instrument prodded into the clay as she bowed away, sawing the phrases of chamber music which were judged by ornithologists or musical authorities to be just such as would induce a reluctant nightingale somewhere in the nearby scrub to strike up and burst into song in sheer emulation.

We had no nightingales in the industrial stretches of south-west Lancashire where I had my childhood home, nor in the precincts of Rugby. The song was only known to me at second-hand through the works of the many poets who had extolled the beauty and romance without attempting to describe it, and when first I heard it over the wireless I was disappointed. I thought the curlew an infinitely better singer, perhaps because he knew just where he was going. But many an evening I sat expectantly when the announcer faded out the programme and said that we were going over to the Streatley Woods to see if the nightingale would sing.

Sometimes it would, more often not, but there was something so improbable, so utterly and unselfconsciously English about the whole enterprise
that I loved it. Television would have ruined it by leaving nothing at all
to the imagination of the listener. I could sit back and imagine the Streatley
Woods without ever wondering where they were. And – though that did
not matter – I imagined them wrong. I had not yet seen them in their
glorious steepness, cascading down the scarp toward the sharp curve of
the Thames where it narrowed for the run-up to Goring Lock. I had not
yet glimpsed them ghostly white with hoar frost on a morning of early
March, the shimmering crystals of ice on the leaves touched by the flame
of the rising sun downstream.

March would not have been the season for nightingales, but on summer
evenings I would sometimes walk across the line of carefully painted needle
weirs from the Goring side to take the track up from Streatley village into
that magical woodland, just to hear the nightingale alive. I never succeeded,
but that did not matter either. I was to hear many in later years, especially
along the Canal du Midi and, greatly to my surprise, in the woods near
the royal palace of Ulriksdal in Sweden, for I had no notion that these
warblers ventured up into Scandinavia. And if I never heard the nightingale, I found the Thames woodland, age-old in its stately beeches, just as
wonderful without them.

It is a curious fact that a river often gives a wrong impression of the
countryside through which it flows. In their more famous reaches the
Rhine and Moselle seem to be flowing between high hills. But this is not
true. Climb the apparent hills to their tops, and the land is found to stretch
away almost flat for miles in every direction. It is just that over a few
millions of years the rivers have cut deep down into the rock and provided
themselves with high banks. It is the same with the Thames. The Streatley
Hills are not quite the hills they appear to be from down on the water,
but a somewhat raised area in a rolling countryside, abruptly sloping down
to the water where the river has forced a passage. So, when one has climbed
to the top of the Streatley ridge,the wood opens out to meadows falling
only gently away to the westward, to a view of fields and copses, of fat
cows keeping the grass at bay and gulls wheeling behind a tractor, leapfrog-
ging each other to have the first pick of the wire-worms and leather-jackets.

Yet the Streatley Hills persist in demanding to be thought of as hills
by the boatman at their foot, and very alluring they are at any season of
the year. In midwinter the lower slopes are often hidden from view by
the fog that lies thick in the river valley, whilst the top of the ridge basks
in clear, pale light. Or sometimes a mist is drifting through the beeches
and the droplets coalesce on the twigs overhead to fall upon the sodden
leaves below so that a muffled, mysterious dripping pervades the whole
woodland. Another weekend early in the year and the leaves will be crisp

with frost, and a light dusting of snow will be criss-crossed with hurrying tracks which show that the wood is by no means so deserted as it might appear. Mice and voles, birds large and small, beetles, a scurrying hare perhaps and a stealthily trotting fox, all leave their footprints in the scrub or on the pathways. In early summer the cuckoo will still be there, and the yaffle laughs heartily as it shoots swiftly out of the edge of the trees, flying low with dipping flight as though its motor were failing.

On just such a summer day I walked up the village street of flint and brick houses hung about with wistaria, and across the main road to take a track that climbed diagonally through the woodland, a path grey with a sticky mixture of chalk and rotted leaves. At the top the wood gave way to a meadow of short grass with all the flowers of the chalk trying to present an alpine garden in miniature. Dianthus grew there, a yellow rock-rose reflecting the sunlight, milkwort blue and pink, and the purple field gentian. There was another bluish patch too, and this was not the field gentian but *Anemone hepatica*, a relative of the wood anemone but with a shorter stalk and a more inquisitive upturned face. It belonged to woodland rather than to a meadow, but there it was, just as if it liked to escape into the sunlight. I was standing still and admiring it when I heard a rather harsh voice, and turning round saw a group of girls in school uniform doggedly marching up the slope ahead of their mistress.

"Now, girls," the strident voice rang through the stillness. "Don't forget, if you see anything unusual pull it up, roots and all, so we can have it in the classroom on Monday. There'll be a prize for whoever can find the most."

It was fortunate that the teacher's voice was so loud. The nearest girls were still thirty yards away down the slope. I was sure that by sheer numbers the gentians could survive the attack of the massed forces of enlightenment but I was worried about the little patch of *hepatica*. I just had time enough to strip my jacket and cover most of them. I lay down on the remainder, appearing to bask in the summer sun. To reach the stile the girls had actually to step over my legs, and some of them apologised pleasantly. So did I. And it was with relief that when two years later I returned to the Streatley Woods I found the anemones still there.

Goring, across the water from Streatley, was one of our church stops. We belonged to the Congregational church at Highgate, for I was brought up as a congregationalist and it was, so to speak, in the blood. But even in my congregational days I had a feeling that theological battles, which had already been won two and a half centuries earlier, were still being vigorously fought, and so if I very naturally wanted to take time on a Sunday to acknowledge with others the brillant design, the love and care in the world which I could explore aboard *Commodore*, I did not feel chained to that one particular way of churchmanship. And it was the

Thames which gave the opportunity to experience the simple reverence and sometimes the very tedious and rather vacuous sermons in village churches.

Our churchmanship was dictated by considerations which were not always very ecclesiastical. Hurley's church was within easy reach of the mooring by the lock. At Abingdon one could bring *Commodore's* nose right up to the wall beside St Helen's. At Bisham there were the remains of a water-gate to the church where one could moor fore and aft to a couple of tombstones and step straight off the boat into the precincts. In the Chapel Royal at Windsor one might sit in the stalls of the Garter Knights and have a seductive illusion of momentary grandeur. Yet, from all those years during which I steered *Commodore* along the course of the Thames, two church occasions have remained especially vivid in my memory. One was Easter morning at Goring.

By tradition, and very naturally too, Easter is a time of re-awakening, of revelation, of thanksgiving, of everything good and hopeful, and it must be for this reason that more is done to decorate the church than at other times, quite apart from the modern habit of bringing Easter gifts of eggs and garden produce for old people who cannot be there. But never have I seen a church burst out in glory on Easter morning as did the parish church at Goring the time we strolled up from the boat when the bells began to ring. It was, of course, the height of daffodil time, and from font to altar the whole nave was lined with sheaves of daffodils, the window-sills and pediments bursting with primroses from the woods across the river, set in moss. Cream and yellow, without a single flower of any other hue, the whole church was shouting its joy for that brilliant occasion. No formal flower-club decorations marred the harmony, no clever use of bark and dead branches; it was a simple breathtaking mass of gaiety and thanksgiving expressed in ordinary local flowers by those who felt what Easter was, and meant it.

The other occasion was at Remenham, a hamlet which hardly exists. It is no more than a collection of farm buildings under the elms (though these may now have gone) and a tiny church so tucked away and humble that one can steer up and down the magnificent regatta reach below Henley without even noticing its existence. It was a midsummer week-end and *Commodore* had lain overnight against the splendid curve above Hambleden mill. The sun was up early, and so were the birds. A heavy dew still sparkled on the cuckoo-pint and clover, and the traffic on the road beyond the meadows had not begun. The air was cool and fresh, laden with that indefinable smell of river which one can so often sense when near a weir. I decided to swing the dinghy off the stern deck and row up to Remenham for the early service. It seemed unlikely that there could be one, but I knew the Church of England to be bound by certain rules which probably included a seven o'clock communion at Remenham even if there were no congregation. I have never been addicted to the habit of holding communion services on every possible occasion, such as seems to beset much of Anglican practice, for I think the event it too great, too full of meaning to be mass-produced and swallowed in three-times-daily doses. But now and again in sheer thankfulness I must go.

Remenham was one of these occasions. I jumped down into the dinghy and set off to row upstream. As I passed the stately Greenlands, now a staff training college, I saw two men crossing the lawn to untie a skiff and set off in the same direction. They evidently had the same idea as I had. That was the total congregation, apart from the wife of the young incumbent who took the service. Never have I known it better done – or perhaps it might be the case that I have never been more receptive. It was the service of 1662 (the endless droning of the 'Alternative Service Book' had not yet been formulated as a soporific) and it seemed to speak to the whole community. Outside, the slow clop-clop of hooves told that the farm horses were getting ready for the first loads of the day, the cattle were calling patiently from their stable, the hens were engaged in the chattering gossip of the new morning, and the pigeons were alternately flapping noisily and cooing in peaceful monotony. And against this natural background of rural sound which had been the same for hundreds of years, Cranmer's splendid phrases came fresh and full of power as the early sun shining through the colours of the window behind the altar flecked the western wall and even ourselves in gorgeous hues of red and blue and gold.

Teddington Lock

II
On Thames broad, aged Back

I t was on an afternoon of downpour in early spring that *Commodore* was ploughing her way against the muddy current of a Thames in flood, and drew in to Shiplake Lock between Henley and Reading. A village policeman was standing on the lockside, and he wrote down the name of the boat in his notebook. Pencil in hand he approached, and paying no apparent attention to the water that rose over his boots he enquired in the most courteous fashion where I intended to pull in for the evening and whether I should be there all night long. This was something I had not as yet decided, and it was so unusual an enquiry that I asked equally politely why he wished to know.

Because, he said, H.M. Government had ordered that the national census, due to be taken that very night, was to be made complete by counting all those not at home. Travellers in the sleeping-cars of long-distance trains would be counted up by the attendants, but the regulations also required that gypsies, vagabonds, wayfaring tramps and the like were to be enumerated by the local authorities. Many would in any case be unable to read a census form (though he quickly added most apologetically that this did not apply to myself) and so all this ragtag and bobtail of tramps, tinkers, persons aboard the *Commodore* – and no doubt the itinerant chair menders, I thought – all these were actually to be sought out and visited personally by a registered and duly qualified enumerator.

I truthfully answered that I could not give a precise location because of the flooding, but it would be somewhere between Reading and Goring.

He nodded. "Thank you, Sir. That will be sufficient, provided I can report which side of the river you will be."

"It's hard to say," I replied. "But why does it matter?"

"Because, Sir," he explained very respectfully, "Berkshire is on that side, Oxfordshire this side. They are two different census areas, two different authorities." Even though I lived far away in Middlesex it seemed that the correctness of the census would be vitiated if *Commodore* and those aboard her were missed out because of some doubt as to which county she was lying in.

The ludicrous nature of the situation aroused in me the little devil that has always a tendency to come out of hiding when dealing with officialdom. "Probably we shall anchor dead in the middle of the river," I said, and with an indulgent sigh the officer wrote it in his notebook. Then he wished us a pleasant voyage and cycled away into the rain.

Dark was falling as we came up to Whitchurch bridge. The lock beyond it was closed, and as I could not be sure whether the river would rise further or would fall away and leave us stranded on the bank during the night I was obliged to do what the fiend had so airily suggested. Nosing up to the central pier of the bridge I put four lines around it and the boat lay happily in the current shadow. Two bunks were in Oxon, I reckoned, and two in Berkshire. Water taps were an important item on the census forms, and I considered them all to be on the Oxford side of the demarcation line in midstream.

After supper I lowered the dinghy and rowed across to Pangbourne on the Berkshire shore and trudged through the rain to the police station. I drew a detailed sketch-map of our position, and the constable studied it thoughtfully. "Looks as if it might be in our area, or it might not," he suggested.

"Exactly. But more accurately it's all in your area at one moment and altogether in Oxfordshire a few seconds later". And seeing he was puzzled, I pointed out that the boat was continually on the move, swinging on the current.

The constable thanked me for demonstrating this awkward fact, but he could think of no way out of the difficulty.

"What is the crucial moment?" I enquired, anxious to help. "I mean, the precise instant when it must be determined in which county how many of us are asleep?"

He looked through a file of instructions. "It does not specify a crucial moment," he said sadly when he came to the end. "It only says 'where the night is spent'."

"Well, would you settle for midnight?"

He regarded me with a trace of suspicion, as though there were a trap. "What if we did?"

"Well, you could get an enumerator from each county, and wait for us to pick up the wireless time signal for midnight. Then they could fight it out. Of course they might need to bring surveyors with them to establish the exact line of the boundary so that ....."

He picked up the instructions and stuffed them in a drawer. "It says nothing about boats," he declared firmly, raising his hand to pull shut the enquiry window.

"But I *want* to be counted."

"I can't help that."

"Please, please. I am only trying to assist the authorities. If we are not included in the census the figures will be false. The assessed numbers of water taps will be seriously wrong." Plumbers might be discouraged and strike for higher pay, I suggested. The unions ... general strike ... rioting ... civil commotion ... bloodshed. Stones thrown at the police.

He weakened at this. "I'll phone the enumerator at Newbury," he said gently. "It's only fifteen miles and she may have a bicycle. She can deal with you. How can she reach you?"

"Tell her to hoot like an owl, and I shall row over."

"Right." He swiftly closed the window, and I returned aboard. We kept a watch until half an hour after midnight, but no owl was heard. Something dark floated past on the flood, but when I speared it with my barge pole it turned out to be only a willow log. As far as H.M.G. was concerned we had ceased to exist.

★ ★ ★

The Thames is a river along which many contrasts are packed into less than two hundred miles. Not all stretches are beautiful, and if the suburban sprawl of Walton-on-Thames may be a handy area in which to keep a small boat and own a week-end cottage none could stretch the language so far as to call the multiplied result attractive. Yet beauty is not just a matter of being old and quaint. There is splendour in the bend by Battersea Power Station, power in the view of the Woolwich Barrage as seen from an aircraft dropping down the flight path to London Airport, a certain stolid defiance about the brick warehouses near Cherry Garden Pier downstream of Tower Bridge. If the pier is still there – for things have a way of disappearing overnight under the planner's hand or the accountant's pocket calculator – it provides the finest of all the views of London, looking back up the reach to the Tower itself and the glory of the City in St Paul's.

I have always admired the matter-of-fact wharves about Tower Bridge, hiding in their name the memory of King Olaf of Norway – Saint Olaf, pronounced with an 'oo' in Scandinavian, so that it was easy enough for the end of his saintly title and much of his name to be shortened to 'Tooley'. He came in 1014 as an ally and wrested London from the Danes, but only Tooley Street and St Olav's seamen's church now recall his visit. The cranes of Tooley Street stood erect like herons wondering where their next meal was to come from, but now and again they had the chance to lean out, pluck the bales or flats from a Dutch coaster and swing them to the landings inshore. Another favourite of mine used to be St Katharine's Dock, but that was in the days when one could take a small boat in through the gates, pay a few pence, and lie untroubled against a bombed wharf amid a riot of rosebay willow herb and ragwort. The basin has now been developed, and very well done too, to provide moorings for visiting yachts. It is complete with shops, restaurant and all the fittings, together with an increase in dues to more than one thousand times what they were when I paid for *Commodore* to lie there. When that change began to take shape I transferred my custom to the Regent's Dock at Limehouse, where the dockmaster was so kindly and welcoming as to allow *Commodore's* successor to have a wharf all to herself, except for a few inquisitive town rats, at no charge at all.

Indeed the charm of the Thames lies partly in its variety. The Henley Reach with its grey-beard church tower, four square and confident by the splendid bridge; the high ridge of the Cliveden woods, the enchanting backwaters below Abingdon, the long, low shoreline of the estuary half-hidden in haze with the white-plumed stacks of cement-works, all these have a quality of their own which is as English as the middle Rhine is German.

It is more than twenty years since I took a boat up to Oxford, more than thirty since *Commodore* felt her way as far upstream as the limit of navigation at the entrance to the long derelict Thames & Severn Canal, and I launched the dinghy and rowed the next four miles to Kempsford, where the depth of water and my muscular energy faded away. It is easy to look back with a sigh and think that times have changed, the countryside is ruined, the hedge-row flowers extinguished by selective weed-killers, the air heavy with the drift of fumes from a nearby motorway, and yet there is a timelessness about the Thames which is not so easily obliterated and however much the larger towns of Britain may have suffered a change – often for the better – the real English countryside seems to have a stability which not even the flight of light industry from the cities is able to upset. And, of all the places in the valley where one can experience the Englishness of the river and its surroundings, none, I think, can surpass the stretch from Shillingford Bridge up to the next weir at Day's Lock.

I first stopped at the bridge below Day's Lock for the practical reason that there was only five feet of headroom beneath the bridge itself. The river was in flood and would need a few days to return to normal, so I had no choice but to put a line or two around the girders and wait, and to spend the time exploring. It was in that way that I came to know and to love Little Wittenham Wood, which slopes up from the river to open out into a short stretch of ploughed land before the summit of the Sinodun Hills – or Wittenham Clumps as they are called locally. These hills had already been visible for an hour of voyage, sometimes to port, ahead or even astern as the river twisted and turned on its slow approach to Oxford.

The Sinodun Hills are real hills, and it was in spring that this flood gave me the opportunity to know them more intimately. The bud scales

were splitting on the trees of Little Wittenham Wood, and the frail first
leaves were stretching up toward the springtime sunshine which came and
went with the passage of clumpy clouds. The same might have been seen
in a hundred other woodlands, where colours would have been no different,
and yet there was a timelessness, an age about this particular wood which
made one hardly dare to speak, and then in no more than a whisper. I
cannot say why this piece of woodland always affected me in this strange
way, spring and winter alike. It was as though in the soft contours and
the mixture of trees it bore a silent witness to the slow, inexorable forward
movement of the geological time-scale and the almost imperceptible evolu-
tion of the landscape in its infinite beauty whilst men hurried by overhead
in jet aircraft to grow old and die and be forgotten.

Sometimes I have wondered seriously whether the wood was not enchanted. If fairies indeed lived in it – as they are said to have done – they
have selected an excellent home, for fairies are known to enjoy wild flowers.
In the stillness of summer when the river is smooth enough to mirror the
trees standing on their heads in front of the bank, then the yellow loosestrife
gazes up at the sky and the heavy bells of the comfrey hang in every shade
from creamy white to orange, dull red and purple. Earlier the floor of the
woodland is a cascade of bluebells following on the heels of that loveliest
of wild flowers the primrose, and when the wild crab apple and cherry
burst into blossom the bees move from flower to flower to carry away the
blobs of nectar, some no doubt to the hives of villagers in Little Wittenham
or to Dorchester across the fields beyond the river. And always there is
the swift repeated burring tap of the woodpeckers which pause to inspect
the human intruders and perhaps fly swiftly away with a flash of red crown
above their black and white.

On one of the first occasions that I roamed through the woodland I
heard a much slower tap-tap-tapping. Silently stalking the sound so as not
to frighten whatever animal it might be I came out into a clearing where
a group of men sat in the shelter of a windbreak that they had fashioned
of stripped bark held between a pair of hurdles. For it was hurdles that
they were making, and several stacks of their finished products stood
leaning against trees ready for carrying away. The heap of stripped bark
and a pile of chippings showed that they must have been there for some
time already.

The hurdle-makers were swift and skilled. A stem of willow-scrub or
beech or chestnut would be taken and deftly split along its length. By eye
the hurdler would judge the size of slot needed in the stouter upright to
take the slat, and then with a tool like a sharp apple corer he would cut
out two holes an inch or two apart. Taking up a chisel he would tap-tap-tap
with a mallet, the wood between the holes would be excised and all was
ready to receive the slat, the point of which might be slightly tapered with

a knife. Two uprights, five horizontal slats and diagonals from corner to corner, and when all had been tapped into place with the mallet a hurdle was ready, ready for use on the downs at lambing time.

I wondered if these were the last hurdlers there would ever be. Perhaps their forebears had come there for centuries already, sitting in the clearing to tap away before moving on to another woodland, just as these did. For the men were craftsmen. They could make a smooth white hurdle for sheep or cows more quickly than a timber yard with all its modern equipment, and yet I felt sure that their trade was heading for extinction, for the electric fence with its single wire and induction coil had arrived. The hurdle-makers would vanish, but the woodland would go on, year after year. And perhaps the fairies would dance in the moonlight in the clearing that had fallen silent, until some soulless engineer managed to fulfil his dream of slicing the whole hill away for a six track motorway and flinging a huge single span bridge over the river.

Not that the hurdlers, medieval in the trade they plied, were the first inhabitants of those slopes, for far back in post-glacial times others (perhaps their ancestors) had certainly peeled off the bark and trimmed smooth the shafts of saplings, not to make hurdles for the farmers but to serve as shafts of primitive hoes and of spears for hunting. The woodland would have resounded then with the gaiety of children and the chatter of men long before English history began ever to be recorded, and smoke rising from the trees would have marked where the tips of the shafts were being hardened by fire.

Their hilltop settlement must have given those neolithic dwellers on the Sinodun hills a good view of impending attackers. For they must have expected attack, otherwise they would hardly have gone to the trouble of constructing so massive a fortress camp with vallum and fosse, scarp and counterscarp and a defended gateway through the ramparts. It is the slightly lower of the twin hills which is fortified, but each carries a central grove of beeches (the 'Clumps') and it is difficult to believe that these were not sacred groves throughout many thousands of years, places of fear perhaps, or possibly of dim dark rites of long ago.

The ramparts in springtime flash with cowslips, but curiously enough the space between them and up to the edge of the crown of trees is land which seems always to have been cultivated. And this gives an unexpected bonus to the visitor, for however tiresome it may be to have to tramp over a field of furrows the annual ploughings turn over the soil where once these early ancestors had their dwellings, and the rain then washes the earth from the pebbles and leaves them clean on the ridges between the furrows. The first time I walked up to the Clumps I wandered up and down the field and picked up seven fragments of earthenware, one of them decorated with little pieces of pink quartz, then a number of bones of assorted animals, and a good flint spearhead with carefully indented edges still sharp enough to cut the fingers. And no doubt one can still glean in these fields, just as one can pick up Roman shards across the river, along the footpath leading to Dorchester, though these come from a rather later period in the history of the valley.

Lying in the sunshine on the short grass of the chalky rampart below the clump of trees one can only wonder how the landscape would have looked in the time of those earlier people. It would, I think, have looked as utterly English as it does now. The river would not have been very different except for lack of the simple barrage below Day's Lock and the sly shade of a rural steamer drifting patiently in midstream to wait the opening of the lower gates. The horizon would have been clearer, devoid of the cloud of deadly sulphurous smoke from the motor industry which an unwise university senate permitted to develop in Oxford. Here and there wisps of smoke would have indicated not the foundries and workshops of Didcot railway junction but the fires where the men were hardening arrows and women busy with cooking.

But what were they cooking? These people who lived on the Sinodun hills for so many centuries, clinging to the thread of life that led from the Neanderthalers to the dawn of our history in the Roman invasion and the attacks of raiders from the North, how did they survive? As yet there were no rabbits in the English woods, but perhaps there were hares. Certainly there were deer, and one good stag could provide a lot of meat which could be smoked to keep for weeks or months. Anything that moved could be used to swell the larder, caught in a trap or shot down by good marksmanship with bow and arrow. Water-voles might not have been the best of prizes, but the river certainly yielded juicy freshwater mussels, to say nothing of crayfish. And then there were always the river fish themselves which could have been speared, driven in to a shallow pool built for the purpose and worked perhaps by the boys and girls of the community, or caught on a neatly worked barbed hook of bone on a coarse tackle of dried gut or sinew. There would have been birds, and in springtime the eggs and nestlings. Snails too, for the edible snail is even now abundant there, and roasted in their shells with wild garlic or onion they might have provided an excellent savoury.

Yet the diet must certainly have contained vegetables as well as flesh. Maybe the tubers of water lilies were not indigestible, and the woodland which then would have covered much of the country was rich in wild apples and cherries, the nuts of hazel and beech and chestnut. The open land had its wild parsnips and carrots, and maybe these as well as grain were also sown in cultivated patches inside the ramparts and outside. Life was hard, especially in winter, but it was probably no worse than elsewhere. Probably things went on very much the same, with hunger alternating with plenty, laughter with crying, contentment with fear, until those who escaped the slaughtering by the eventual Roman armies fled into the depths of the wilder country toward Wales and faded out of history, leaving the Thames unchanged behind them.

★ ★ ★

In these early days in command of *Commodore* I learned much about the sheer loveliness of the upper valley at all times, whether in sun or rain. I loved it by day, or when running the long and twisting reach below Hambleden in the dark, or when the lock-cuts had ice enough for our passage to be accompanied by a sound like that of breaking glass and we had the river entirely to ourselves. But once a year we would go down river all the way to Teddington and enter the tideway. The object of this trip was to see the Universities Boat Race.

The Port of London Authority was noble enough to put down strings of moorings along parts of the course from Putney to Mortlake and one had merely to write to them and have a numbered location assigned. There was no charge for this remarkable service, which had the advantage for the eights that private craft were kept out of their way and they did not have to dodge drifting boats which had dragged their anchors in the tide. Every year for five years we applied for a buoy and had a position granted to us.

At that time the idea of navigating tidal water with a strong stream filled me with a certain apprehension. Apart from the original run up from the Medway it was a new experience, and even if it taught me valuable lessons for later and more enterprising voyages the mere fact that if anything went wrong with her single motor *Commodore* would proceed up or down river borne on the tidal current alone was an awful one to contemplate, especially as tugs, strings of lighters and even Dutch coasters could be encountered as far upstream as Isleworth and even occasionally above Teddington Lock. So the Friday evening before the Boat Race was invariably spent moored to the piles below the weir at Teddington, where I would busy myself with cleaning the fuel filter, checking the ignition system, and generally crawling about in narrow spaces with a minimum of comfort. Next morning we would slide away from the berth to head for Richmond barrage and the frightening great unknown.

On the first occasion the tide was running out and when we reached the half-tide lock at Richmond I could see that the foreshores ahead were well exposed, so I timorously asked the lock-keeper if he thought there would be enough water for our modest draught of less than three feet. He laughed pleasantly.

"Water enough? Plenty, Sir. Just follow that steamer down to make sure of the channel."

The steamer was a spanking affair which had taken off from Richmond landing stage for a day at the races. She was so loaded with passengers that there was no room for all of them to sit down, and she must have had twice our draught. She came into the lock behind us, so when we had dropped to the lower level I drew aside to let her pass, then followed in her wake, trailing her a mere thirty yards astern. She was running fast, but at top speed I could keep up with her.

I was just considering what an elegant building Syon House was where it lay beyond the meadows to port, and morbidly recalling that it was there that the body of Henry VIII burst in its coffin so that the dogs licked up the drippings, when the trusty *Commodore* leapt upward like a horse taking a fence and came down with such a thump that all of us aboard fell forward and some of the galley saucepans noisily announced that they had done the same.

If a boat drawing less than three feet is hard aground it is safe enough to roll up the trousers and drop over the side, which is what I now did. The water came nowhere near to my knees and I could walk right round the ship on a shoal. With the water still going down I had a fear that the vessel would fall over on one side, and later I was grateful to this first stranding for teaching me that such a worry was unfounded. As for the Boat Race, our visit would have to be postponed until the following year. The tide had still hours to run out, and it would take as long again before we would be floated off the shoal.

We had not long lain there when a tug came chugging by. He was a big, fat fellow, and the marks on his bow showed that he was drawing between eight and nine feet.

"You ain't standing, surely," said the skipper, leaning out of his wheelhouse only a few yards to our side. "They've just dredged this reach down."

By noon I could walk right round the ship on dry land, and I took the opportunity to examine her hull. A couple of herons watched me from the shore, looking disdainfully down their long noses. From time to time a string of lighters would come past, heavy laden with coal for Kingston power station. One of the tugmasters nodded sympathetically.

"That bank shouldn't be there by rights. But the tide's turned now. A couple of hours and you'll be off again." Then, as an afterthought, "Cambridge won by three lengths," he shouted as he chugged on his way.

Next year I was determined not to be stranded on a shoal which had no right to be there, so I let the main run of shipping pass down the river and only set off from Richmond when the tide had already turned, so that if by any chance we went aground we should be floated off within minutes. There was plenty of water and we had passed Syon House and the Brentford Reach when quite unexpectedly the engine gave a sudden jerk and stopped. Putting it out of gear I pressed the starter and the motor ran perfectly,

On Thames broad, aged Back
35

but as soon as I tried her ahead the engine stopped dead. Some unseen hand was holding the propeller from turning. There was nothing for it but to drop anchor, change into bathing pants, hang on to a rope and disappear under the side of the hull to see what the trouble might be. That was easily discovered. Around the blades of the propeller, the shaft, the rudders and the brackets was a mass of stout rope such as the lighters used, wound tight with all the force of *Commodore's* seventy horse-power and packing the entire space between the propeller shaft and the hull.

I recall thinking that the Thames early in April was not only murky but much colder than I expected. There was a strong stream running by now, which made it more difficult to hang on with one hand and work a hacksaw with the other, so the task of cutting away all the coils of rope took more than two hours. I was just climbing back on board when the authority's tug *Winston* came steaming past us with a blackboard mounted on her side announcing that Cambridge had again won, this time by three quarters of a length.

Next year I took every precaution and even went down river the previous afternoon. We picked up our mooring, spent a somewhat disturbed night because of the rocking which so mysteriously accompanies the change of tide at high water, then sat on deck next morning in a stiff breeze which was driving sharp waves along the river. I was keyed up with satisfaction at being in position, and on such a good berth that we should be able to watch the whole exciting contest from Duke's Meadows almost to Mortlake brewery. But no eights ever came. Oxford had sunk in the waves, and the umpire had ordered Cambridge to stop.

I happened to mention this succession of disasters to one of those curious rough characters who are at home on ships and lighters but – to put it in a somewhat Irish way – very much at sea when on land. He had great knowledge on all matters connected with shipping, though probably that knowledge was not invariably correct.

"It ain't natural," he said thoughtfully. "Every time as you goes to the Boat Race something happens like. No, 'tain't natural, that it ain't. There's something wrong, something as didn't ought to have been. Did you *never* see the race, then?"

"Only once," I said. "And that time we had a nasty accident of a different kind. It was this year."

I explained that at Teddington we always picked up a friend, Howell Nicholas, who had stroked a college boat at Oxford some years before and was a keen oarsman. On this last occasion we had reached our allotted mooring off Duke's Meadows, and sure enough the eights came racing up the river almost level and rowing splendidly. As they came past us there was not so much as a canvas between them, and Howell climbed on to the roof of the after cabin, yelling himself hoarse in his hysterical encouragement of the Oxford crew, waving his boat club scarf in the air.

The eights were as usual followed immediately by the umpire's launch, the BBC commentator John Snagge and his technicians, a boat load of old blues who held some privileged position or other, and finally by five large steamers crowded with passengers and running at such a speed that they set up as tremendous a wash as the tidal bore on the Severn.

"Get down," I shouted to Howell. "Get down, or the wash will throw you overboard."

He shook his head, cheering wildly. "Row up, Oxford! Row up!!"

"Look out," I yelled. "Hold on!"

But the warning was too late. The first big wave took us on the beam and *Commodore* rolled heavily. With a startled cry the Oxford supporter fell over backwards and disappeared head first into the stern well. By good fortune he was not even concussed, just somewhat bruised and shaken. But he was lucky, I said.

"Hm." The ancient mariner seemed in his simple way to be considering. This feller you had along, the one as nearly killed himself, was he with you each time?"

"Why, yes," I said. "We picked him up at Teddington each year. As a matter of fact he was a minister."   ·

"A minister! Did you say a minister?" The old salt stared at me in amazement.

"Yes," I said. "He was our minister in Highgate."

He stared incredulously. "You mean, not a proper church vicar like, but one of them non-conformist fellers?"

I nodded. "Yes, he was a Congregationalist as a matter of fact."

The sea-dog looked at me with a mixture of pity and wonder. "How was it as you didn't know better than to let a minister set foot on your ship? Lucky to get off as light as you did, I'm telling you. I wouldn't go on a ship with one of them aboard, not for a hundred quid I wouldn't. Everyone knows as it ain't safe. They brings bad luck. An' you not knowing that!"

I tried to take in his explanation of our troubles, but there was at least one obvious flaw in it, I thought.

"Come off it, Charlie," I said. "Are you seriously trying to tell me that the time the Oxford boat sank it was just because we happened to have a Congregational minister on board round the next bend? I don't think that makes sense."

"You may think as you pleases," he said gruffly. "Only it was you as carried a minister aboard, and it was you as never got to see the race except the time he nearly killed himself. Ministers may be all right on land, but afloat, never. They always brings bad luck, no matter how it strikes."

The Meuse in flood at Ecluse St Joseph.

Regent's Canal Dock. The new *Commodore* waits for the tide – and the European waterways.

The Boat Race belonged to the upper reaches of the tideway, but having come all the way down river for that occasion I would sometimes take *Commodore* right on through the heart of London, just to experience the greatness of the city and the magnificence of its turgid river in a way I could never have done ashore. And it was in the evening that the scene was at its most beautiful. In the early fifties the Pool of London was not yet dead, and at times it was bustling with traffic. Big ships were on the move at the top of the tide, and even at low water the river was alive with the hurrying tugs of the lighterage companies. Ashore, the lights, red and white on the opposing lines of road traffic, moved slowly ahead in a long trailing queue and even in midstream one could hear above the noise of the Embankment roadway the massed twittering of the starlings returning to settle for the night among the planes. The great buildings of the riverside stood opulent and confident, the Tower of London was bathed in soft floodlighting where it lay dignified and formidable on the port hand. Then beyond the mighty chains and towers of Tower Bridge the grandeur suddenly gave way to an older riverscape with coasters standing on campsheddings where sailing ships had lain before them, the ranks of cranes stood erect before the brick warehouses with rows of double doorways in mid-air, and in the background the trim spires of Nicholas Hawksmoor and Christopher Wren stood out faintly against the last light of evening. Long trails of solid creamy smoke drifted across from the power stations, beautiful enough for a painter but carrying in secrecy a deadly load of sulphur dioxide to kill the silent woodlands and poison the lakes in countries a thousand miles away. Inns appeared here and there, dipping their ancient toes in the line of high water, the Yacht and the Gun, the Duck and the Mayflower, the now fashionable Prospect of Whitby. Beyond, blocks of soulless council flats rose into the sky as though trying to reassure the population that the sterile uniformity of the sociologists was indeed gradually replacing the bombed sites and the ricketty terraces of a Limehouse that was slowly becoming extinct, or at least changed beyond recognition.

But Limehouse Basin – or the Regent's Canal Dock, to give it the more elegant title – was still a W.W. Jacobs scene. It was a run-down kind of place, for canal traffic was slight and the quays were frequented more by elderly ships picking up scrap metal for export before they themselves were written off to join the pile. And frequented by rats, fat and watchful for the Limehouse cats. The water was oily, littered with the great floating islands of rubbish that seem to appear from nowhere in docks and never leave them. A few tar-stained herring gulls dipped into the blackish water to salvage edible scraps, and groups of dumb lighters and empty barges clanged heavily together in whatever part of the dock the wind had for the present cornered them. Not made fast to anything whatsoever they were like abandoned waifs, and rather unattractive ones at that.

The last time I put into Limehouse at high water we shared the lock with a Dutchman of some fifteen hundred tons. He came from Delfzijl, I remember, that being a port on the Dutch side of the Ems estuary to which *Commodore* had already been when bound for Scandinavia. The ship had come to pick up a load of old iron. When the inner gates were slowly wound back the way ahead was obstructed by a score or more of lighters, some with a lighterman leaning against the tiller motionless, hands in pockets, cigarette a-droop.

"Let the Dutchman out first, Sir," the dockmaster called. "He'll clear a road."

And so he did. The skipper opened up and ran straight into the pack at full speed. Bump, thud, bang, crash, thump, the lighters were quickly scattered and we followed close astern of him to our berth in the corner nearest the entrance to the Rotherhithe Tunnel entrance, while the dismal dock echoed the reverberating collisions between the scattered craft.

Beyond Limehouse I rarely strayed unless bound for other lands. The dock was a good place to lie, and between there and the sea there was no possibility of mooring for the night. It was only later that I came to know the bleak, grey skyscape over the dim receding shores of the estuary, and to relish the glow of phosphorescence in our wake on a summer's night as we rose and dipped over the wash of the incoming ships on our way toward other waterways in other countries.

The London river

III

K. and A., and G.U.

T he pigeons, busily engaged in picking up the chunks of stale bread and
    grains of maize thrown to them by visitors to London, gave a quick
glance at the marching column which was passing across their private
feeding ground of Trafalgar Square, then returned to their pecking. Like
all the best and most English of demonstrations the little group of marching
men was orderly, and both proud and a trifle embarrassed as it made its
way through the streets of central London, flanked by four smiling policemen and watched with mild interest by the citizens on the pavements who
clearly approved of democracy and the right to conduct a properly regulated
and peaceful demonstration but were not quite sure what it was all about.
And no wonder, for as we marched stolidly in fours down Charing Cross
Road and through Trafalgar Square, and the police politely held up the
traffic for us at every road crossing on the way to Berkeley Square, the
placards we held and the slogans we occasionally shouted were neither
highly provocative nor easily understood.

"Hands off the K and A!" What on earth, one might well wonder, was
or were the K and A? Perhaps an onlooker with an exceptionally deductive
mind, if he happened to notice that the man marching beside me had a
broad leather belt in which was stuck a cranked winding handle, might
have realised that the implement was a lock windlass and that the individual
was a canal carrier. As for the K and A, he could hardly have been expected
to know that the letters stood for Kennet and Avon Navigation.

We marched, all thirty of us, to the Ministry of Transport. Two of our
leaders were allowed inside to present a petition, which probably came
out again unseen a few days later in the weekly load of waste paper. We
then disbanded, and that was that, though the rumblings of which this
scene was a part were to continue for a quarter of a century until their
goal was to some extent realised. The Kennet and Avon Navigation was
restored over much of its length, very largely by sheer hard work and
volunteer navvying.

If the Thames was *Commodore's* home water it was also her training
ground for further adventure, and within two years of her maiden voyage
up river as a mobile weekend cottage she began to push her nose into
other waterways. For the Thames connected with several of these, and if
the Thames and Severn Canal was derelict, the Oxford Canal too narrow
in the locks, the Wilts and Berks Canal filled in and abandoned, and the
rivers Wey and Lea too low under the bridges, that left three connecting
canals which had reasonable dimensions and were still in use. They were
the Kennet and Avon, the Grand Union, and the Regent's. It was the first
of these which immediately attracted me, for chugging up through Reading
one could not fail to be intrigued by the murky river which flowed in,
past grimy gasholders and heaps of coal, to debouch (a pleasantly descrip-
tive word used in Pilot books) under the main line railway bridges into
the Thames.

Curiosity led me one day to turn into the Kennet and proceed cautiously
round the gasworks to see what lay beyond. I knew this had once been
the main transport link between London and Bristol before the coming
of the railways, but that was all. I had never seen a boat of any kind
debouching from it, so I sounded with a long pole, only to find that the
Kennet was so deep that I could not find the bottom. Soon we were passing
up a walled river with half a street on either side very much as one might
in Belgium, and around another bend came in sight of a trim lock, spick
and span in its paint of grey and white, and with a splendid show of
daffodils along the edge of a neatly trimmed lawn. This, however, proved
to be a Thames Conservancy lock named Blake's Lock, giving access to
the Kennet and Avon Navigation which, strictly speaking, only began just
beyond it. Little traffic passed Blake's Lock, but the keeper said we might
certainly go through as far as the wharf at High Bridge. That was handy
for shopping. But further we could not navigate, he said. The bridge
beyond was far too low. During the war it had been reinforced by putting
girders underneath it. Further ahead the canal was in a shocking state and
at Devizes, where there were twenty-nine locks in succession to descend
to the valley of the Avon, the whole affair was said to be derelict.

Shortly after this I had occasion to go to the West Country. The Cornish
Riviera Express thundered into Reading, swung away to the valley of the
Kennet and followed the waterway for nearly forty miles, often within
yards of it. I stood in the corridor, watching in fascination. I saw one lock
after another, one or two of them lacking a balance beam or looking forlorn
and unused. There seemed plenty of water and on the river were a number
of swans, and moorhens beyond count. Here and there the cows were
standing in the edge of the water, but apart from one sunken barge with
reeds growing through the rotted planks I never saw a boat. In fact —
though I did not know it at that time — one forlorn but determined com-

mercial craft was still running between Reading and Newbury, the *Colin*, skipper John Gould.

Before Pewsey the railway swung away to the south, but the effect of that half hour of high speed travel along the banks of the waterway was enough to make me determined to try at least to reach Newbury or even Hungerford by this canal which passed through so pleasant a countryside and which looked (at least from the train) to be in tolerable condition. But I had to find out about the waterway, and the only fact I could discover was that it had been bought many years back by the Great Western Railway, which had slowly run it down because it was a potential rival. The Great Western had, I knew, just been nationalised to form a division of British Railways, so I telephoned Paddington Station and asked if it were possible to take a boat through the canal. The official I spoke to laughed. He seemed to think the question one of the more amusing that had come his way for some time.

I repeated the query and he realised that I was serious. No, he said, we could certainly not go through. For one thing, there was an obstruction under a bridge at Reading which reduced headroom to four feet and seven inches. When I suggested he could get the obstruction removed he laughed again, which was hardly surprising, for the obstacle was a mass of solid steel girders set into the buttresses of the bridge. I tried to reason with him, to be kind, sweet and amiable. Then I became unfriendly, annoyed, incensed. I even said I took a very serious view of the matter, which was true – even if it made no difference.

It was the somewhat scornful attitude of the official which aroused in me a determination to enter the K and A, and perhaps marked the beginning of my wanting to pursue a course up closed waterways wherever I could, and only as a last resort to take No for an answer.

I was thirty-five at the time, and that is an age when obstinacy has a tendency to reach a level from which it may or may not descend later. The fact that I received such a brushing off from an official in Paddington station made my blood pressure rise temporarily, but in the long run this was to prove of great benefit to several waterways, notably in Sweden, and perhaps also to the K and A itself.

Walking down Gower Street in Bloomsbury I happened to notice a brass plate on a door: "Inland Waterways Association". I had not previously heard of this body which at that time was in its earliest youth but was already energetically fighting the closure of canals. If the Inland Waterways Association had not been founded by Robert Aickman just in time, Britain would probably have no more than one third of the waterways which today are still open or have been restored from dereliction to be used as excellent amenities for the many thousands of boatmen, hikers, anglers, painters and bird-watchers who can now enjoy them.

The IWA knew all about the pitiful state of the K and A. John Gould with his narrow boat *Colin* was one of their members, and he kept them well informed. Soon after I had taken out a membership it was realised that it would be an excellent thing if I could fight my way through to Newbury as I suggested, for although Gould was regularly forcing a passage and keeping the canal at least nominally in use his craft was not very high above the water and was sufficiently narrow to be able to use the locks if only one gate at either end was capable of being opened. *Commodore* would provide an excellent challenge to reluctant authority because she needed most of the eight feet six inches headroom guaranteed by Act of Parliament when the K and A was built, and she was beamy enough to need both gates to be swung.

Full of enthusiasm in my imagined role of a waterborne St George rescuing the fair damsel K and A from the wicked intentions of the railway dragon I settled down with pen and paper to write three letters full of threatenings and slaughter. The first was to the Divisional Engineer, telling him in peremptory fashion that on a certain day in April I would be entering the Kennet in order to voyage to Newbury and back. I would expect, I wrote, to find all the canal works in good order, and to suffer no hindrance or delay. His reply was exceedingly friendly; the engineer set out the small dues I would be required to pay, and went on to say that although the navigation might prove difficult in some sections every effort would be made to pass us on our way with the least possible delay. The canal staff had already been informed of the voyage and instructed to give every possible assistance. He even ended by wishing us a pleasant and enjoyable trip.

At the same time I wrote to Stirling Cables, a company which had a works at Aldermaston. IWA intelligence had reported that they had put a pontoon bridge across the canal, secured to the bank at either side. In fact this was a sensible idea, because it enabled their own workpeople to cross the water to work instead of having to walk all the way up to the next road bridge, but canal enthusiasts saw it only as a quite unauthorised interference with navigation, and so that was the tenor of my letter. Once again I received a disarming reply. Nothing could be further from the wishes of Stirling Cables than to delay us for an instant. If I would be good enough to notify the time of our arrival a man would be stationed on the bank of the canal to watch for me and remove the bridge instantly.

The key to the whole trip, however, lay in the obstructed bridge at Reading, so I despatched a letter bristling with rectitude to the Borough Engineer. It told him that we needed all but ten inches of the statutory headroom, and I had heard tell that the Borough had illegally reduced this from eight feet and six inches to a mere four feet and seven inches by obstructing one of the bridges. If this were so, then the obstruction must be removed, or suitable steps taken to allow a boat of seven feet eight inches above the waterline, with the decks cleared, to pass. Even to this letter I received an immediate and charming reply. The Deputy Borough Engineer would personally be at our service, it said. We had only to telephone the town hall on arrival and he would attend to the matter at once and ensure our passage. It was impossible to remove the obstruction under County Bridge because the bridge itself was resting on it, but we need have no anxiety. We should be passed through without difficulty, and the writer would like to take the opportunity of wishing us a very pleasant and successful voyage.

So once again we turned into the Kennet and passed the area redolent of coal gas and biscuits to the quay we had visited before. From a phone box I called the Borough Engineer, who was as charming as his letter had been. His equally delightful Deputy arrived, and explaining that beneath County Bridge the river was very deep he gave orders for all the sluices to be raised at Blake's Lock so that the reach would run out and the level drop. I stripped the windshield and lowered the dinghy off the cabin top, then all we needed was to wait until the water had fallen away sufficiently. It took a few hours to do so, for the river was flowing rather more than normally because of the wet weather earlier in the week, but at last we could chug cautiously under the girders beneath the bridge and up to County Lock. This was no smart affair with a keeper in white cap and brass-buttoned waistcoat but a sad structure with herbage sprouting from the timber of the gates, water trickling round the heel posts and the brickwork crumbled and mossy. Yet the paddles worked easily enough, especially when worked with the double-length windlass handle I had prudently had constructed by a blacksmith before embarking on the trip. Just above the lock a dredger was moored. It was piled with steam coal but was rusting away where it lay, having apparently decided that it was unequal to the task of keeping the waterway clear and would prefer to die quietly and in peace without getting up steam.

The first few miles of river were a surprise. The water was clear, the flicking tails of green weed pointing to its purity, and the next two or three locks worked so easily that I began to wonder where the sections were in which navigation might prove difficult. But I did not wonder for long. On the side of one of the locks three men stood dismally in the rain, awaiting *Commodore's* arrival. They had been detailed by the divisional office of the nationalised waterways system to accompany us all the way to Newbury. They had brought with them coils of rope, a spade and pick-axe, wrenches, a couple of crowbars and as much equipment as one might expect of a mountaineering expedition. The men piled all the gear on board but politely declined the offer of a lift to the next lock. They would get there more quickly on foot, they explained. And in that they proved right, for although *Commodore* once or twice came near to catching them up she was always halted by a bed of reeds or a bank of mud which needed repeated attack before she could force a passage through it.

It was now that I encountered for the first time the turf-sided lock, a speciality of the Kennet. Instead of a brick chamber there was a shallow form of brickwork, from which the locksides sloped away, not as walls but as gentle grassy banks. A line of railway rails secured to uprights ran down each side of the centre of the lock, above the brickwork, to keep a boat roughly within the correct area, but this meant that as the lock filled there was no means of stepping off the boat unless into several feet of water. The sloping sides also increased the area that had to be filled before the gates could be opened and, because nothing had passed through the lock since the last time either the *Colin* or another narrowboat belonging to an enterprising carrier named Knill had passed that way a few weeks earlier, the ground had become somewhat drained out. Although all the paddles were opened and the Kennet was doing its best to fill the pen the water level only rose very slowly over the grass. How many thousands of gallons were needed just to saturate the earth banks I could not guess, but until the whole structure was thoroughly waterlogged it could not be filled to the top level. The process was made even slower because holes made by water-voles and moles on one side of the bank sometimes connected accidentally with burrows of rabbits on the other, so that when the water had at last risen to near the top level there would be a spurting and gushing as a torrent of water and mud surged out into the field below. This the canal staff dealt with very easily, merely jumping on the source in their gum-boots until they had squashed it and sealed it.

The need to draw off such quantities of water before a lock was filled had another disadvantage. The water was taken from the reach immediately ahead. Shallow and silted as it often was, the mere fact that we were approaching dropped the level of the canal by sometimes as much as half a foot, and this under conditions when every inch mattered. Sometimes we had to borrow water from even further ahead to make our passage over the mud, and so when we called a halt for the evening above Theale Bridge, six miles up from the canal entrance, it not only gave the canal men a chance to return home by train, but allowed the pounds to fill up again overnight.

I was surprised to learn from the friendly canal gang that the waterway not only had 106 locks – many in the central section being derelict – but no less than 48 swing bridges, a number of them on the section up to Newbury. At Theale three riders sat on their steeds, patiently waiting for us to swing the bridge back into position again after passing, and that was something we could do with reasonable speed for the bridge crossed the river not far above the water and so was low enough for Gould to have had to swing it every time he passed that way, and for Knill to manœuvre it when he brought his cargo of salt all the way from Cheshire. The difficulties came with the bridges which lay high enough for these narrow-boats to pass underneath them in the closed position. Such bridges had not been swung for several years, and probably not since the Admiralty made the ridiculous and expensive decision to transfer a pinnace from side to side of the country by way of the K and A. That was during the war years, and paralleled a decision by the Germans to move a similar craft from the North Sea to the Black Sea through the Ludwig's Canal in Bavaria, which was in much the same condition as the K and A. By a curious coincidence I met the skippers who had been assigned to the command of each of these absurd enterprises. In either case the result was the same; an expensive ship had to be written off as damaged beyond repair.

The swing-bridges of the K and A had on either side of the roadway a post several feet in height from which a steel bar sloped down to each corner of the bridge on that side. These bars were cut at one point and the ends threaded, one part of them with a reversed thread. A sort of collar was fitted over these ends, and if it were rotated it had the effect of shortening the rod, and so turning up the toe of the bridge at that corner. When all four rods were slacked off, the frame of the bridge sat solidly on the abutments, but the mere act of shortening all four tie-bars by turning the collars had the effect of buckling the bridge so that its toes lifted clear of the abutments. The whole affair could then be swung out of the way, but of course if the bridge had not been moved for several years the threads were rusty, the beams of the roadway had become tired and settled down to a long and undisturbed sleep, and the whole bridge stuck its heels in and resolutely refused to move.

Firstly we had to find the long iron lever for turning the collars. This was usually hiding in the long grass nearby, or beneath the fallen leaves of the last autumn, but sometimes no amount of heaving and pushing would turn the collars, which through long disuse had rusted solid. How-ever, the canal gang were equal to any such simple problem. They had bricks, crowbars, sledgehammers and wedges, and they would force up the ends of the bridge so that I could place *Commodore's* padded nose against the roadway and let her push with all her might. By the end of the second day I had become quite accomplished at bridge-moving, and it would have needed a remarkably obstinate bridge to stop our progress.

Our approach to Aldermaston was immediately noted by the intelligence system of Stirling Cables, and the man who had written us the courteous letter drove down to the lock, introduced himself and took the family off to buy groceries, bread and milk. Like others he was so full of willingness to help that I felt embarrassed at having written in such pompous and demanding terms. But I was already discovering something which was to be an experience repeated on other waterways in other countries, namely that those who live by abandoned canals become exuberantly enthusiastic when there arrives at last a boat determined to force a passage against the years of neglect. And it was at Aldermaston also that I discovered how to bring an irresistible force to bear upon an immovable object, in this case the road-bridge.

Somewhat exhausted by a day in which we had covered rather less than five miles in nine hours and finding the road bridge apparently immovable I sent the canal staff home for the night. By the volume of traffic which unexpectedly appeared at supper time heading from north to south, I realised that the bridge was on a commuter route. These motorists were returning home from Reading after a hard day at the office either there or in London. The *Schlaumeierinstinkt*, as the Germans so aptly call it, began at once to work in me, and next morning I was up early to put a couple of heavy ropes across the approaches to the bridge, marking them with fluttering rags to prevent them being run down. The drivers of the first few cars halted had a tendency to complain, muttering about missing the eight-forty up-train and so forth, but soon the realisation spread that the quickest way to Reading Station would not be found by turning round and threading a roundabout route of country lanes but by taking off the jacket, rolling up the sleeves and getting to work. Within a few minutes I had halted enough cars to provide a work force that could have moved anything, and when the canal gang arrived with extra tackle to deal with the bridge they found us on the upstream side of it, patiently awaiting them at the bankside.

It is not necessary to make a lock by lock report or to catalogue all the difficulties we had to overcome before reaching what little was left of the once extensive quayside at Newbury. We averaged just over four miles on each day of the four-day struggle from Reading, and the lock-keeper at Newbury town lock broke into tears when we drew in sight. Never had he expected to see a boat of such size and such good looks appear at the foot of his lock, which had been virtually unused for years. Like others, he loved the canal which had been the scene of the whole of his working life. There can be nothing more frustrating than to put loving care and work into something which one knows will never again be used, and maybe in this case there was also the feeling that our arrival at Newbury wharf was the first rift in the clouds of closure and nationalised abandonment which hung over what had once been one of the great achievements of that fine Scottish engineer John Rennie.

Throughout our stay at Newbury the rain fell. I welcomed it, because it swelled the Kennet so that it rose up its banks and spilled into the fields. We had at least a foot more of water than on our upward journey and this made the going easy. We ran over the mudbanks and shoals as though they were not there, and as we had already shifted the recalcitrant bridges they opened more easily. The entire journey back through the seventeen locks to Reading was so easy that we accomplished it in a day and a half. For the last few miles we could even manage without the help of the three stalwart maintenance men, and when County Lock came into view I felt a momentary wave of relief. It was indeed momentary, because looking past the lock I could see that instead of being the customary four feet and seven inches above the surface of the water the girders under the road bridge were almost awash.

I dropped two anchors astern, each with a tripping line, and hailed the girls in the brewery office beside the weir pool to be so kind as to telephone the town hall and say that *Commodore* was waiting to pass the bridge. I quite expected the Borough Engineer to say it was impossible, but not a bit. Everything would be done. The charming Deputy himself came to the scene to superintend operations. Blake's weir was opened down to the last pin, County weir was obstructed with more boards laid across the top, though this latter only helped for the few minutes before that reach had risen to the new level. The river dropped somewhat, enough for me to ease the bow under the bridge by working the trip lines.

By mid afternoon it was obvious that the river was not going to fall enough, so I stripped off the navigation lights, ventilators, and anything which projected more than an inch above the cabin top. I also partly scuttled the ship by opening a sea-cock and filling the bilge as far as I dared, which was an inch or so below the starter cable which ran under the engine.

By four o'clock we had achieved much. That is, Reading had uncomplainingly shut down its sewage filtration plant and the waterworks, the water intakes to both of these being now exposed. I wondered at the long-suffering, uncomplaining readiness of the corporation to go to unlimited trouble and expense in order to get a boat from one side of their bridge to the other, and it was only later that I realised that there was more to it than sheer helpfulness. Reading had wanted for some time to have their bridge over the Kennet replaced by one more suitable to the quantity of traffic it had to carry, but at that time permission to build a new one had to be obtained from some government department or other and the relevant department had turned down their application. To Reading the visit of *Commodore* was extremely welcome, as it provided ammunition for the next round of salvoes in the battle for a new bridge. The more trouble her visit caused, the better, and I suspect that it was no accident that one of the first arrivals to view what was happening under the bridge was a reporter. And a kind young man he was, too. He had brought his own cake for tea, and he generously shared it with the ship's dog Susan.

It was nearly five o'clock when I was asked to climb up the rope-ladder

I had rigged to the bridge and talk to the Town Hall by telephone. It was by now obvious that no further measures could be taken to drop the level of the river any more. Too much water was coming down from further up river, and after so much rain this was only to be expected. However, if we would wait until morning a mobile crane would arrive from an RAF Station and load ballast blocks aboard the ship until she lay six inches lower in the water, which would enable her to clear the girders.

This idea was a good one, but it prompted me to produce an even better. Why go to such trouble, I asked, when we could load ballast aboard so much more easily? Surely the simplest way would be to load the boat with Town Hall officialdom.

The Engineer agreed that this would perhaps serve instead of blocks. How much weight did I need, he asked.

Half a ton would do, I thought, so he said he would see what he could do. He would do so at once, as the staff were already leaving for the night.

And so a little later taxis began to arrive at the bridge, and one by one those of the Town Hall staff whom he had managed to catch were helped up to the parapet and down the ladder to be stowed as far forward as possible, for from amidships to the stern we were well clear of the girders. One of the men was a really fine specimen and must have turned the scales at fifteen stone or more.

My estimate of half a ton proved too low. With all available bureaucracy stowed aboard I could see that we still needed at least two inches more. However quite a crowd had now collected to see why these men with briefcases and bowler-hats were queueing up to disappear over the edge of the bridge, and there was no lack of volunteers. A policeman had arrived to control the traffic, and he stopped a trolleybus which had for conductor one of the heaviest and largest men I had ever seen. Along with one or two passengers he slid down and we packed them in.

By now the accommodation was full to capacity and yet we still needed perhaps a quarter of an inch. Word was sent to the lock keeper just behind us to close the lower gates and open all his top paddles. This would deprive the flow over the top of the weir of one lockful of water. The effect would only last for two or three minutes at most, but it was worth trying.

From the stern I watched the man close the gates, then wind fast at the rack and pinion gear. Then he raised his arm to signal that he had done all that was possible. Looking forward I saw that the boat was dropping, and at last a glimmer of daylight could be seen between the girders and the cabin top. Lying flat on the fore-deck the Deputy saw the light too, and moving slightly to one side to trim the ship he called to me that she was clear. Very cautiously I pulled the trip line on one anchor, then the other. Silently, with less than a quarter of an inch above her, she drifted through to the quayside, and the life of Reading began to return to normal.

The K and A should have been enough to frighten me off canals for ever. Instead I got waterways on the brain, and only two months later I was nosing into the sad-looking approach to the Grand Union Canal at Brentford. There was plenty of traffic in those days, and I was in time to encounter one of the stranger habits of British water transport before the advent of containers, aided by the pigheadedness of union organisers, dealt the London docks a mortal blow and at the same time extinguished the traditional trades connected with it.

Dickens once wrote of the Thames lighterage that it was "the very type of blundering obstructiveness and an excellent example of how time is allowed to be wasted in this country". Half a century later things had hardly changed, but as lighterage is now almost extinct I am happy that I was in time to see it operate, without being sunk.

Ships in the Pool of London or the docks would be unloaded over their sides into lighters or 'dumb' barges, the word not describing the skipper or lighterman but the fact that the craft were devoid of motive power. A laden lighter weighed perhaps eighty or a hundred tons, and several would set off for Brentford behind a tug. Approaching the tidal cut which runs from the river to the first lock of the Grand Union the tug would put on top speed and give a toot on the whistle, at which all the lighters were cast adrift while the tug swerved away to stay in the river. The lighterman on each barge would then show signs of life for the first time since leaving dockland. In sole command of a massive and somewhat dented hulk proceeding at several knots he had merely to lean on the tiller to steer into the cut, a matter of no difficulty at all. It was then that the blundering obstructiveness began, for he had to bring his lighter to a halt before the lock, and this he could only do by colliding with the walls and quaysides or any vessels which happened to be moored to them, his sole weapon a long barge-pole of the kind one would not touch anything with. Or, he would crash head-on into a similar craft coming in the opposite direction, for at high water lighters could also leave the canal, and to propel them out of the lock a line was attached to them and pulled powerfully by a capstan on the lockside to get up a good momentum. Some of the dumb barges coming out of the canal empty had no crew at all, it being presumed that they could not reach the river without being brought to a halt by a head-on collision.

Our own progress up to the lock was difficult. I did not wish to have *Commodore* sunk by these massive craft out of control, so I had to wait for a chance and then run a few yards to the next safe gap between moored craft further along the wall, then spend another half hour or more in fascinated observation of how the commerce of London's shipping was conducted, and all the while thinking how fortunate I was to see for myself the system Dickens had written about.

While waiting to reach the lock I had the chance to see the other form of lighterage operate, a trade now gone for ever but in the mid 1900s something one could see any day on the London river. It was the monopoly of licensed watermen and needed great skill. At the low water turn of the tide a lighter would be cast off from the Pool without a tug of any kind. The lighterman had a single huge oar or 'sweep' at the stern, and as the craft drifted up the river he had to keep it heading for the bridge holes and clear of moored vessels. With good judgement he could make Brentford before the tide turned, and there his most difficult moment came. Unlike a lighter cast off from a tug his ship had no way on it relative to the water, so using only the sweep he had to bring the craft over to the outside edge of the curve and out of the tidal flow at exactly the right moment so that it would glide to a gentle halt in the canal cut, provided of course that nothing got in the way or obstructed the entrance, for at that time the Brentford cut was busy.

Sometimes in London I would stand on Westminster Bridge and admire the slow, broad strokes with which a lighterman kept his craft heading through the bridge arch and avoided the run-back on to the piers. It looked so easy. Robert Louis Stevenson once wrote that he could not see why a bargee should ever die, and he would have thought the same of these London watermen, gliding proudly and without obvious effort up past the Houses of Parliament and the palace of the Archbishop of Canterbury to deliver a haystack of esparto grass or a cargo of pulp to Brentford. In the docks I once had a chance to talk to a lighterman named Ron, who told me of his first attempt to take a lighter from Waterloo to the Grand Union. At Brentford he was too late in crossing the stream and the flow carried him on past Isleworth and the "London Apprentice", through Twickenham Bridge and the Richmond Barrage, nearly to Teddington. There was no anchor aboard, no means of stopping, nothing to be done but to avoid all the yacht moorings and keep going. It was, he said, a lovely day and he enjoyed it. He saw parts of the river he had never visited before.

Eventually the tide turned and he used his sweep to turn the lighter. Back he went through Richmond, and he was ready to turn into the canal. He took the lighter within feet of the bullnose, but the ebb was faster than the flow and so he missed the entrance again. He reckoned it was impossible to get in on the downward flow with the cut set at such an acute angle to the stream, he said.

A few hours later he had passed Westminster and the Waterloo lighter moorings from which he had taken off in the morning. When the ebb had finished ebbing he was down river near Greenwich. It was eight hours since he had eaten his sandwiches but he had no chance to go ashore to a pub. It was beginning to get dark, so he lit a lantern (the lighters usually had one in case they finished a run in the dark) and set off up river again.

It was chilly in the night, he said, and he had no coat, but the prospect of making Brentford by one o'clock in the morning cheered him up. This time he cut over earlier and he only missed the entrance by a yard or two. Once more he visited Richmond, and though on the second run downstream he made a desperate effort to propel the boat into slack water at Brentford it was no good. Dawn saw him down at Battersea.

At this point I interrupted his tale and asked him why he had not asked for help from a tug. There were always one or two lying in the stream or at the Brentford wharf, but I saw from his expression that the question was foolish. He was a newly licensed waterman even if it were his first trip. He was not going to look ridiculous by asking for help. He would deliver his load at Brentford if it took him a week. And eventually he did. Twenty-eight hours out from Waterloo he came drifting in to the Brentford cut. He was so hungry he could have eaten a horse. And it was not a very profitable trip either, for as a licensed lighterman he made the delivery for a flat rate of payment, which was not particularly generous either. I think he said it was seven shillings. There was no overtime or nonsense of that kind to induce a waterman to spin out the hours.

The last of the skilled lightermen has long disappeared. And so have the horses. When *Commodore* passed the Brentford lock she found herself trailing lighters which were bound for the paper mills twenty miles and twenty locks ahead, slowly pulled along the canal by dear old horses which knew every familiar yard of the way and slackened speed when approaching a lock without being told to do so. In fact the horses seemed to me to be much more competent than the unskilled hands who lounged against their tillers. But not all the craft were lighters. This was still the era of the narrowboat.

The reason why commercial traffic became extinct on most of the vast network of British canals has little to do with railway ownership or narrow-minded ministry officials. The system was absurdly uneconomical. The canals of England formed the first considerable network in the world and they were built too early. Too early meant too small, so that the English barge skipper and his wife were moving only thirty tons of cargo, or if they had a butty (trailed boat) seventy. His continental counterpart even in the days of horse-towage was moving five or ten times as much. Enlargement of the English canals might have saved the narrowboats, but it was thought of too late. The approaches to towns were built up, there were too many bridges at the eight foot level, the hundreds of locks on many waterways were so narrow that in those early days I would jump across them. The chance to rebuild the waterways to European dimensions had gone.

But in 1950 the narrowboats, seventy feet long by seven feet broad (compared with the French *péniches* of one hundred and twenty-five by sixteen, with double the draught) were still plying the cut in their dozens, and all through Hertfordshire and up to Warwick we would hear the characteristic pop-pop-pop of their oil engines. Samuel Barlow Coal, Fellows Morton and Clayton, Grand Union Canal Carrying Co, their painted roses bloomed on the doors, the imaginary castles stood proudly on their panels, and the brasswork gleamed. And the boat people themselves were courteous and amiable, in no way resenting a private boat navigating for pleasure. They had pride, too, and pride was probably necessary if the eleven foot by six foot space in which one lived and reared a family was not to become a diminutive slum afloat – which is just what it had been until George Smith successfully campaigned for the passing of the Canal Boats Act of 1877, which laid down certain minimum standards.

Commodore's trip up the Grand Union was made six years after Tom Rolt's *Narrow Boat* was published, the book which first put canals on the map of public imagination, and there were now less narrowboats on the move than when he made his famous trip of exploration in the English midlands. But they still seemed prosperous. Their people had their own habits, too, of which the best known was to decorate the ship with exquisitely painted roses and castles. Shortly before our voyage the government decreed that all narrowboats were to have their scrolls and hearts of red and green painted out, the roses and castles to be obliterated, the beautiful hand-painted water-cans to have their loveliness scrubbed out. Everything from stem to stern was to be painted in the blue-bag blue of national ownership, with a permitted straight-line edging of yellow. It is hard to believe that any bureaucrat should be empowered to strip the family home of others and kill all their decor and individuality, but that was the case. If I could have discovered who was responsible for such an idiotic and heartless instruction I think I would have forced entry to his home and painted his wallpaper, furniture, windows, pictures and everything to hand in the same horrid blue, or maybe bilious green, just to see how he liked it.

However, the canal people were not to be cowed so easily, and within weeks of the fearful overpainting the colours began surreptitiously to creep back. Government Gill Sans lettering gave way to twiddles and flourishes, bouquets of roses appeared illegally and deliciously, and the painted cans appeared once more. Nowadays these are sought-after souvenirs made for the tourist trade, but in 1950 the can was still for real use. And it was beautiful, because simple people such as canal boatmen often have the natural human facility for wanting beauty in the things of everyday life, and being willing to pay for it.

They had other traditions too, and when invited aboard their boats I had the opportunity to notice them. One was a big bow of pink crepe paper hanging somewhere in the cabin. Nobody knew why it was there, but it was unthinkable not to have one. Another tradition of pride was the lace-edged china hanging dangerously on hooks inside the hatchway. Often inscribed with words such as "A Present from Coventry", the plates had pastoral scenes and flowers and were of good quality. They were never used except perhaps for a birthday or wedding, and were not cheap to replace. One young woman on a narrowboat at Fenny Stratford told me she was going to hunt around in the Paddington junk shops when she reached London, to replace breakages. They would cost her two pounds apiece, she said, "But you can't be without the china, can you now?"

Perhaps the life-long lack of a garden was compensated by the painted roses inside and out, but most of the craft I went aboard also had flowers in a vase. Never wild flowers, which were to be had everywhere for the picking, but only the very best would do. Boat women did not hesitate to walk into a florist to buy the blooms. The choice seemed always to be the same: six of the best carnations.

So this voyage was in narrowboat territory, and all the way to Warwickshire we met narrowboats engaged in their regular trade of carrying. Some were taking coal from the Midlands to London, others were carrying coal from London to the Midlands. A few carried bales of paper, or bricks, and the Ovaltine boats had a freight of something I took to be feed for the Ovalhens which roamed the hillside above the canal near Hunton Bridge. They were a part of the English scene, these narrowboats, and in their old-fashioned lines and decor they suited the winding, simple course of the canal with its short flights of black and white locks and canalside inns far from anywhere. The whole scene was a century 'and a half old, and the England of the canal had a beauty all of its own. And the Grand Union also had two tunnels, the Blisworth and the Braunston.

Tunnels are common in England, because so many of the waterways cross a watershed from one river valley to another. Partly to save excavation and also because it was difficult to haul a horse out of the water if it fell in, they were rarely povided with towpaths. The horses went over the hill and the boat under it, propelled by 'legging', a well-known curiosity of British canal life. Two men lay on planks rigged out from the sides of the boat and pushed with their legs on the walls and ceiling. The diesel engine put an end to legging, but when it was practised there were professional leggers also. A boat needed a man on either side. One would be the boatman, the other a legger.

George Smith, the great fighter for better conditions on boats and the education of the sixty-thousand children in their cabins, described in *Canal Adventures by Moonlight* how he met Ben the Legger, then aged eighty-six, who had legged through the Braunston Tunnel for more than fifty years, "that is, he has lain on his back upon a narrow piece of board about 12 inches wide and 3 feet long, overhanging the side of the deck, called a 'wing', and worked a boat along with his feet between 50,000 and 60,000 miles, or twice round the world, through this watery and ghostly cavern of black midnight darkness."

Though Smith was the pioneer fighter for the boat people he was not the only one to care for them. Canal families, as on the Continent, tended to live a life cut off from much contact with landsmen, and so the London City Mission had opened a place at Brentford with a warden who was a general friend and adviser to the boat people. Every year he used to approach me and one or two others to help finance him as Father Christmas. Sometime in the third week of December he would set off northward to try and visit every narrowboat between London and Braunston which had children aboard, and produce a surprise for them. It was a delightful and happy idea of his and it lasted until the boats disappeared, unable to compete with the road hauliers. Then poor Father Christmas was forced into retirement, to look back like others on the days when the pop-pop-pop of a boat could be heard round the corners of the woodlands or echoing down the Braunston tunnel.

Up the locks, through the two tunnels of Blisworth and Braunston and down another flight we came at last to the waterways junction and inland port of Braunston. Nowadays this is a vast marina complex with boat showrooms, moorings for hundreds of private craft, workshops and everything connected with the enormous increase in inland boating and the money to be made in catering for it. But in 1950 there was not a yacht or cruiser to be seen there. Narrowboats were lying two or more abreast all along the cut, men were cleaning the sides, women polishing brass, boat dogs growling or barking, children playing, all living in a world completely detached from that of the A45 which crossed the canal at the bend ahead and which before the coming of the motorway carried the heavy road traffic between London and Coventry and Birmingham. On the wall of a small warehouse beside the lane which led from this road to the dock a faded notice still declared that "Steamers leave here daily for London and Birmingham", though it must have been many a year since they had done so.

Braunston Dock had a little side cut crossed by a 'roving bridge' to carry the towpath. One side had a workshop building and a quay at which we could lie, and along the opposite bank a row of canal anglers sat staring in silence at their floats. At the end of the siding was a covered dock and a slip where a chippy was rebuilding the bottom of a wooden narrowboat and a youngish man deftly painting the illegal hearts and diamonds on the supports for the canvas hold covers. He was watched critically by his master, the elderly yard manager, Mr Nurser.

Obviously delighted that such an improbable ship as *Commodore* should find her way up to his dockyard basin, which was within three miles of the geographical centre of England, Mr Nurser made us thoroughly welcome. We knew of him as one of the two great artists in narrowboat painting (the other being Tooley of Banbury) and whenever he had the chance to leave his office he would walk over to the paintshop, pick up his brushes and set to work on a water-can or dipper with all the concentration of a royal Academician but with much greater speed. Sometimes he would disappear into the cabin of a narrowboat which was being fitted out, and when he climbed out again the doors were resplendent with the traditional scenes of strangely Bohemian castles with a river flowing by, and a bridge, and maybe a range of mountains in the distance.

One morning as I was strolling along the basin on my way up to the village I noticed Mr Nurser standing outside the workshop looking *Commodore* up and down. As I came up he nodded.

"Seeing you come all the way from the Thames, an' I can't remember as I ever knew another boat to do that, an' seeing as you come and stayed here in Braunston, well, if I were to paint a can for you, would you promise me something? Come what may you'd never sell it. Can you promise me that?"

I quickly assured him that nothing would induce me to sell such a treasure. And when later in the day I returned from a walk along the towpath the Braunston can was standing on *Commodore's* hatch, flowery in its shiny new paint.

The Grand Union at Brentford

IV

One more River

"T ake my tip and run her over."

It was quite by chance that I found myself standing on a British Railways Ferry next to Allen. It was a car ferry and I was bound for Oberammergau via Ostend. Allen was heading for a holiday on the Belgian coast. He was the boatbuilder who had reconstructed *Commodore* at Gillingham on the Medway, and after asking if she were still fit and well he came out with this suggestion.

"Take her over. You'll have thousands of miles of rivers, estuaries, canals, anything you like. Holland, Belgium, France, there's no limit. Take my tip and run her across."

Until then it had never occurred to me that our voyaging could be extended further than the English midlands. I had not even considered the existence of waterways in other countries. Boating ended, in my imagination, at the Boat Race course in the tideway with rare and daring thrusts down river as far as the Isle of Dogs and Greenwich. But to cross the Channel – it was as unlikely as a voyage to the moon.

Allen was most reassuring. "Pick a good day, and she'll go over easy as winking. She's a fine boat and will ride anything. Not like this old tub," he added as we both ducked behind the combing when the ferry stuck her nose in the air before burying it in a wave.

All winter his words went round and round in my head. In the spring I began to consider what spare parts it would be prudent to take for our single paraffin engine, and in the early summer I began to study charts. I had always liked maps, but charts were new to me, and every time I came upon one of the symbols *Wrk* with a picture of the front half of a ship sticking out of the sand I wondered for a moment whether the idea of taking *Commodore* abroad was really such a good one. But nothing could take away the dream, and early in the summer *Commodore* was passing through Teddington lock, heading for St Katharine's dock, where she was to load stores.

To cross the Channel in a small boat is something which hundreds of yachtsmen do every week of the summer, but thirty years ago things were different. Small boats had no radio, or radar, and even depth sounders had hardly made their appearance at the annual Boat Show at Earl's Court. In 1951 food was still rationed in England, but the skipper of a small boat going foreign was considered either so heroic or so mad that the government graciously allowed him a licence to purchase enormous quantities of ham and butter, and other things in short supply. With *Commodore* lying at a bombed quayside sticky with the syrup that ran from piled heaps of brown sugar I went with my permit to find Mr Smith. He was an exuberant, kindly man who had his office in a room with "Headmaster" warningly painted on the door, in an old and abandoned school near the Royal Mint. The classrooms were filled with racks of everything a ship could need, from one-ton anchors to tins of toffees, and while I made a selection Mr Smith gave each of the children a beach bucket and filled it with sweets.

The thrill of being able to voyage on continental waterways during the summer school holidays was something I could not have dreamed of. It was the gateway to a world detached from the ever increasing traffic of the land, the hurry and bustle, the tearing down of the old and beautiful to replace it by the modern and practical and – regrettably – permanent and indestructible. Of course there were yacht clubs on the continental coast, pleasant, friendly and unpretentious places, but the marina had not yet arrived. Entrepreneurs had hardly begun to sniff the money to be made out of the boom in boating which was soon to begin. One could come and go without difficulty and after the neurosis of the war years had died away one could be sure of a welcome. Very soon I discovered that even in busy ferry ports such as Calais or Boulogne one could head for a quayside, ask if one was in the way, and sit there undisturbed. Nobody came round to milk the yachtsman for money.

My first foreign voyage however was not to Calais. After a night bumping expectantly against the wall in Ramsgate we left with the tide flowing toward the continent, and in the late afternoon I was steering up past rows of fishing boats towards the gates of the largest dock I had ever seen, the Demeysluis at Ostend. It seemed unbelievable that this vast structure should be put into operation at no charge at all, just to admit *Commodore* to the Belgian canals, but so it was. A welcoming smile, a handshake, and we were there, ready to chug out toward the waterways leading to Bruges, Ghent and Antwerp, and lands of mystery and surprise.

Even on that first inland voyage abroad I discovered that the waterways of Western Europe extended far enough to keep one busy for a life-time of exploration. Naturally I came to have a special affection for certain favourite routes, and perhaps most of all for that which led through Antwerp to the valley of the Meuse, and thence to Alsace, the Moselle,

Switzerland, the Midi or the Mediterranean. In a quarter of a century I came to know it so well that I was more familiar with the Meuse than with the Thames. It had beauty, it had romance and the age-old legends of Bayard the magic steed, it had forests with wild boar and deer, grim fortresses, and little French towns with no claim to fame even at the time of the fearful slaughtering still remembered at Verdun. And it was on that same route that the strangest adventures came my way.

From the Antwerp docks the deep and wide Albert Canal runs almost straight across the sandy heathland of the Campine to join the Meuse in the industrial basin of Liege. It is one of the busiest waterways anywhere, and day and night alike the heavy cargo-carriers and coasters go pounding along it. The only possibility of a night's rest without being bumped on the stone banks was to escape into a side-turning such as the end of one of the connecting waterways where the traffic came to a halt at a reasonable hour. The one I usually chose was the short branch canal leading into Hasselt, but on the third run from Antwerp we had left the docks in the afternoon, and Hasselt would be too far. On early voyages I had noticed a sort of large bay at the bottom of which was a lock. My map showed that this led into the Nethe Canal, which eventually became the river Nethe. This seemed an admirable corner, out of the main stream of the traffic, so I turned into it, prospected cautiously, and chose a berth for the night.

The lay-out of Viersel Lock was in no way unusual. There was a pen some fifty metres long with gates at either end, and to the right and beyond it stood the lockhouse with the toll office and bureau. The whole structure was comparatively modern, for until the coming of the Albert Canal in the nineteen-thirties there was no connection down to Lier, which could only be approached from the other direction, by the tidal estuary of the river Nethe. A minor road led up to the lockhouse, and some way beyond the lock the Nethe Canal was crossed by a modern concrete bridge. Otherwise the land was agricultural, and there were no other houses immediately close by. The upper water level was on the Albert Canal side of the lock, which had a drop of a few metres to the canal level below. I mention all these details because of what was shortly to happen.

The lock was not much used, because very little traffic went to Lier. At seven o'clock each night it closed operations, and it had already done so when we arrived in the bay. Shortly afterwards the lights in the lockhouse went out, and darkness settled over Viersel Lock. There was no sound other than the usual very slight dripping from the gates. The dripping was of course on the side away from us, as it was the custom to leave locks empty at night to retard the growth of weed on the walls.

I had moored *Commodore* right across the gates because the stone sides of the bay sloped to such an extent that it would have been difficult to keep her fended off. The gates met, of course, at a slight angle and did not provide a straight wall, so I secured the bow to a pile outside the lock, and this meant that the open hatch of the stern cabin looked out across the corner of the lock. From my berth on the starboard side I could look out when awake over the top of the gates to a brilliant firmament of stars. My wife had the port side bunk, and two friends slept in the bow cabin which had no direct view of the outside, and none at all toward the stern.

I slept soundly until about one o'clock, when I awoke suddenly. There was a loud rushing of water through the paddles. Something was going through the lock. I turned over and looking up through the hatch I could see the tall mast of a ship in the pen. It carried a bright lantern near the top, and was swaying slightly, as craft usually do when the water surges and swirls in a lock. And it was rising, slowly but definitely.

I sat up, mildly cursing my own foolishness in mooring across the gates. Before they were opened *Commodore* would have to be moved out of the way.

The skipper of the barge called to the deck-hand at the bow to slack off his rope. Several instructions and answers went back and forth, and in spite of the rushing of water against the bow of the vessel I heard them distinctly. They were in Flemish, which was not surprising, as the boats using that minor Belgian waterway were more than likely to be Belgian barges than others.

As I slid out of my bunk the further end of the ship had risen into view. There was a light of some sort in the wheelhouse and I could see the figure of the skipper standing at the stern line. The deck-hand was near the bow on the same side, tending his rope and letting it ease round the bollards as the boat rose. Within another two or three minutes the lock would be full and the ship ready to cast off and come out. We must move at once.

As I struggled to pull a pair of trousers and sweater over my pyjamas I also woke my wife and pointed out of the stern hatch at the ship in the lock. She stared in amazement, then pulled on a dressing gown, saying at the same time that I had better wake our friends in the fore-cabin as we might need their help when finding another mooring.

I ducked under the main beam which ran from side to side of *Commodore* just ahead of our cabin, and went through the saloon to rouse our friends. John sat up.

"A ship in the lock," I said briefly. "We have to move."

"Coming." He jumped down, waking Sylvia in the process. Leaving him to explain I hurried to turn on the fuel, which I always shut off for safety at a cock in the engine compartment.

John had meanwhile looked out of the side hatch and seen the ship with its mast and lantern. So had Sylvia. I climbed the ladder from the galley to the steering position and I was so intent on opening the instrument panel to start the engine that for a moment I did not pay any attention to the ship in the lock or look backward. At the same moment my wife came through the stern hatch to tend the stern line. I pressed the switch and as the motor started I turned round ready to call to her to let go aft. But I did not call. Like her, I could only stare in astonishment. The lock was not full but empty. There was no sign of any ship. Under a clear and starlit sky the lock was entirely deserted and in darkness.

What explanation could there be? It is possible for one person to be half asleep (as in sleep-walking) and imagine something, but it is stretching credibility too far to suggest that four people on board a boat could all see another ship which was not there at all. No amount of cheese or Belgian beer could produce such uniformity of hallucination. Unless I have invented the whole story for the benefit of sensation, or have convinced myself that the three others witnessed the ship in the lock exactly as I did, then there is only one possible explanation. And that is, that the ship with its Flemish speaking crew was there, right there in the Viersel Lock, just as I saw it. And moreover that some five minutes later it had vanished along with a lockful of water, the quantity of which can be roughly estimated as several hundred thousand tons. Vanished into – what, or where?

I was brought up in Baconian tradition and groomed for a career in scientific research. To put it another way, there was no place in my scheme of things for dematerialising barges or disappearing lockfuls of water. Things had to be observable, amenable to examination and measurement. The ship with its mast and light had been observable and so had its crew, at least as far as the sound of their voices. They had been observable in an ordinary way, just as a boiled egg can be seen, but they had not been observable in a way that Francis Bacon would have liked – that is subjected to precise examination and measurement. Yet it was not Francis Bacon who was woken by the sounds in the lock; that was myself. And I am absolutely certain that the ship was not subjective. It was as objective as any ship can be, and even thirty years afterwards I could describe its lines and appearance in the greatest detail.

One could continue to dissect the affair for pages and be no nearer a solution. Probably one is looking in the wrong direction. The fact is, there is no explanation of this event in terms of science any more that one can explain the uplifting feeling of being on a mountain top. Perhaps the difficulty is merely that in our modern world people are narrowly but definitely trained to pooh-pooh anything mysterious, anything which cannot be grabbed hold of and taken to pieces. Science demands – wrongly, I think – wearing blinkers as far as the strange and not-understood is concerned. It would be quite natural if friends of mine who are scientific (and who in these days is not?) were to say they can only assume I imagined the whole incident, and even imagined that our two friends aboard experienced the ship too. I cannot argue against refusal to believe. I can only say that the incident happened. Even if I were to describe the Flemish ship in some detail, that would gain nothing but an indulgent yawn.

Some years later I passed that way again, this time in *Commodore's* successor, *Thames Commodore*. We had spent the night in Antwerp docks, and after an early start we came up to the junction with the Nethe Canal by midday. This time we also had friends aboard, but not the same ones, and having decided to turn through Viersel Lock to visit the old city of Lier I resolved not to mention the affair of the vanishing barge in case our guests should be worried. It was a hot and sunny day of May, and as I chugged into the lock I had no real expectation of anything out of the ordinary. Four years had passed since the event of the night-time mooring and I had already passed along the Albert Canal in the meantime. I had not forgotten my night-time experience, but being myself disinclined to accept such odd events as real, or as important, I had pushed it to join a heap of other former events in the filing system of my memory.

I made fast in the lock, the gates closed behind us, and the paddles began to whine at the lower end, set in motion by a young *cantonnier* or assistant. And in an instant the temperature of the air dropped from the upper sixties to such a chill that one of our guests – who was a doctor – shivered and went below for a sweater. Everyone noted the extraordinary cold, but it was something more than just a cold damp in the air. There was an eerie, sinister feeling about the place that was indefinable and yet intense, heavy, and threatening.

It was the custom for bargemasters to show the papers and also to give a nominal tip of a few small coins to the keeper of the lock, so I went ashore and over to the office. The man was seated at his desk, and he was shivering so that he could hardly enter the name of the boat in his day-book. Two other men were standing to one side of his table. Not one of them said a word, either to me or to each other. I put the tip on the table, murmured a 'good day', and left. A few minutes later the lower gates opened and we moved out of the lock to head for Lier, G. K. Chesterton's "Lovely city of Lierre". Only a hundred yards beyond the lock we were in brilliant sunshine, and the temperature was back in the sixties once more.

On our return in the evening I wondered what we should find, and I had resolved that if we were late and the lock were shut I would turn back a short way rather than spend the night in so strange and ominous a place. However we were in good time, and yet just as we came up to the bridge below the lock the temperature dropped, the rain fell, and an icy wind blew upon us with such fury that I had to drop anchor in mid-canal. Both banks disappeared from view in billowing fog, and so did the bridge. I hung back on the anchor chain and hooted for the lock to open. I shouted and rang the ship's bell, to no avail. There was nothing to be done but to shiver and wait.

After a while my wife volunteered to be put ashore, to go up to the lockhouse and wake up the keeper, who seemed quite unaware of our arrival. I dropped the dinghy and rowed her to the bank. When she returned she was freezing with the cold. She had deposited the tip, and the three men had looked at her, but none had spoken a word.

Since that occasion I have more than once gone chugging past the bay on my way along the main line of the Albert Canal. Each time I had a desire to turn down into the Nethe Canal once more, but by this time I was sixty and had married again. When I told Ingrid of my experiences at Viersel Lock she at once made me promise never, never to stop there again or to try to go down to Lier. And knowing her to have an exceptional wisdom and sensibility for the weird and unusual, and seeing that she was very serious about the matter, I promised. I have never again stopped at Viersel, and never shall.

★ ★ ★

The Meuse at Liege is a whole day's run distant from Antwerp. Beyond the coke-ovens and blast furnaces and mountains of slag of Liege the river passes through the finest scenery of Belgium, by Namur and Profondeville, Dinant and the rock whence Bayard leapt to disappear forever in the great forest of the Ardennes. Two days up from Liege the course leaves Belgium and the river becomes French. The sophisticated Belgian villages give way to the splendid wildness of the Ardennes forests.

Back in the nineteen-fifties a private boat was a rare sight on all but a few French waterways such as the Seine and the Canal du Midi. Inland voyaging was still in its infancy and the first small hire fleet was only just establishing itself on the Marne. Throughout most of the French canal system one might meet several dozen barges in a day's run but one could travel for a month without encountering another yacht or cruiser. And because private boats were so rare the system of paper-work for dealing with them at the frontier was hazy and far from being standardised.

To enter France at all it was necessary to have a *Permis de Circulation*. This had to be obtained in advance and was issued for any route desired. It was supplied free of charge but had to be shown at every lock and stamped at each "Bureau de Déclaration". If without this piece of paper the skipper had to walk or cycle to the relevant divisional office of the Bridges and Highways to obtain one. That could mean a journey of fifty miles each way, so I was always careful to obtain mine before arrival. It was part of the office-work which necessarily preceded any voyage into

France, work which included securing a *Carnet de Passage en Douane*. Monsieur Zivy, who had opened the hire fleet on the Marne, told me that it would be wise also have a *Certificat de Capicité*, which was a sort of aquatic driving licence issued to bargees. I studied the regulations carefully and found that a written exam was needed as well as a practical one, and that commercial captains were required to provide a certificate from a priest testifying to their "lack of moral turpitude". After closer acquaintance with some of the French bargees I wondered how they managed to secure such a testimony. Presumably the same way as I obtained my *Certificat*; the exams were waived in exchange for a bottle of Scotch.

So when *Commodore* drew in at the French customs quay at Givet I was confident that I had a file of all the documentation necessary to allow us to proceed up the valley and through the waterways to Strasbourg. A Belgian barge obligingly invited us to lie alongside and, as I stepped over the hatches to present myself at the customs hut, the bargemaster wished me luck. It was three days since he had taken in his papers, he said. This was hardly reassuring, but I was still confident.

In the hut I was welcomed with great courtesy and a round of hand-shaking. I announced our destination as Strasbourg, and the clerk took down a box file of regulations and amendments, counter-regulations, annulments and revisions, and searched through them until he found the rules applying to yachts. He studied them, shook his head, and said that we might not enter France. We were to turn round and go back. It was a pity, but the regulations were quite clear.

When I said it was not just a pity but idiotic the clerk looked as though he were deeply wounded and he summoned the chief, who examined the file of rules and confirmed what his junior had said. It was not possible to enter France. Patiently he explained the matter to us.

The regulations stated that one might not enter the country without a particular kind of permit or *laisser-passer*. This had always been the case until a year or two earlier, when in the interests of international travel and to make things easier the *laisser-passer* had been abolished by a decree.

Why, then, I asked, might we not proceed?

The chief then looked sorrowful and said that it was a matter of regret but it was only the *laisser-passer* which had been abolished. Owing to a most unfortunate oversight the regulation which required a ship to have one had not been abolished. It was indeed a pity, but that was the situation. He could not himself amend the rules. The regulation was still there, he said, and he turned the open file toward me and pointed to the paragraph.

I then suggested that if we had to have this permit, and the forms no longer existed, nothing would be simpler than to sit down and type one out. But this it seemed was not within the authority of the chief, and when he told us so a revolt broke out in the otherwise orderly civil service. One of the clerks, a handsome young man in a corduroy jacket began an impassioned speech. What on earth would people think if they heard that visitors, Britons, friends in time of trouble should meet with such obstruction? Did not France beg people to visit it? France awaits you! A noble land for your holidays. France welcomes you! Ha ha! For when you arrive there you are told to go home. You may not enter. No, no, no. What indeed would people think of France – and rightly? Where was the spirit of the *entente cordiale*, of brothers in arms?

The chief made a despairing gesture. It was the regulations, he said. One could not go against the rules. He did not make them himself. But certainly he could not interfere with them. There was one greater than he. And he looked up at the ceiling as though expecting General de Gaulle to come fluttering in on wings.

The corduroyed clerk asked me if I did not think France a land inhabited by cretins. I got round that one by saying that I readily understood that even in such a splendid and desirable land as France regulations might now and again be designed or amended by cretins, but of course the rules were not made in Givet. The friendly clerk indulged in another indignant outburst about the treatment of friendly and harmless visitors, and he was then told to take the day off and clear out.

During the course of the morning the chief telephoned Paris, Lille, Charleville, even the Belgian customs post we had just passed with no more than the wave of a cigar. He tried to get me to travel the two hundred miles to Paris to present myself at the Ministry of Communications, but I refused, backing up my disinclination by reading to him the formidable paragraph on the inside of the cover of my passport about Her Britannic Majesty's Principal Secretary of State for Foreign Affairs requesting and requiring him to allow me to pass freely. The remaining clerk said he thought that clinched it. They loved the Queen, and was she not very beautiful? If the Givet customs refused her request, would that not be a much graver offence than to let us pass? If it became known that the Givet Douanes cared nothing for a personal request, made on behalf of the gracious queen herself, what then?

The chief threw up his hands in despair. I thought he was going to weep, but he did not give in. I then changed tactics and said that if no permit was issued by three o'clock I would go ahead, and if the next lock at Trois Fontaines was ordered not to let me though I would return on my collapsible cycle to Givet and telegraph the Foreign Office and *The Times*. This was followed by a loud cheer from a French barge-skipper who had been attracted by the commotion, and who had just finished a bottle of wine. The queue in the office was growing, for commercial shipping was continuing to arrive and no others could be attended to until our matter was settled, partly because the other clerk had been sent away for the day. Two Dutch skippers winked at each other and to me, indicating that this was what one had to expect. The French bargee gained courage and began to declaim loudly about state parasites, and the whole system of government which was designed solely to charge taxes and obstruct all enterprise. He wrung me by the hand, slapped me on the back and told me to proceed up river and let them try to stop me if they dared.

The scene was becoming noisy, but it was clear which side had popular support. Two men who were plastering the wall put down their tools to come and listen. The chief was obviously concerned that things were getting out of hand but the heavy French bargee could not easily be thrown out. Nor could he be silenced. But just at that moment a dusty-looking hand from a cement barge pushed to the front of the queue. He said he had an idea. The Anonymous Society could adopt us, couldn't they?

The chief of the bureau clutched at the possibility of any way out of the impasse and begged the man to expound further. All the while he looked increasingly relieved, and finally he took up his telephone and rang the Anonymous Society itself in the coaling harbour of Givet. Soon his face brightened. He put down the receiver, and if he again threw up his hands it was now with sheer relief. Yes, the society would fix it, he said. It would cost us three thousand francs, but that would be the end of all our troubles.

"Old francs or new francs?" The French had a maddening habit of using the old quantities even after a revaluation by a factor of one hundred. Three thousand francs could mean three pounds or three hundred.

"Old, naturally," the chief of customs replied.

It was well worth three pounds to be allowed to proceed, even if to pay anything at all was not altogether just, I thought. So I agreed to take the offer, and one of the workmen cycled off with me to the coaling harbour where a number of heavy ships from the Ruhr and the Dutch coalfields lay in the inky water beside the ranges of black hills of coal dust and anthracite. At the offices of the Company General of Fluvial and Maritime Transports Anonymous Society I was provided with a 12 D, a form as large and thick as a parish magazine on which were entered all the data of *Commodore*, her size and age, value and destination. The company certified in triplicate that she was a coal barge under charter to them and that she was bound for Strasbourg in ballast, not having taken on a cargo of coal. Back at the customs hut the chief scanned it, stamped it, and told me we might proceed. He hoped we would enjoy our visit to France. I returned aboard, the French skipper pushed out our bow, the others cheered, and as we set off up one of the most beautiful river runs in all Europe the corduroy-jacketed clerk stood on the bridge to wave to us. He was enjoying his day away from the office.

Voyaging for a week up the Meuse, which at that time was the main route for barge traffic to and from Lorraine, I was able to bask comfortably in the belief that all our troubles were over, and so it was in complete confidence that I descended the magnificent valley of the river Zorn lock by lock through the Vosges toward Alsace. As for other yachts there were none, and even when I repeated the same trip six years later aboard *Thames Commodore* the sight of a private boat was so rare that it caused something of a sensation. Indeed when stopped for the evening at Hochfelden I was surprised by a succession of clattering sounds, the cause of which was that two motorists approaching the canal bridge from opposite directions had both turned to stare in astonishment at the boat, and the result was a head-on collision. One vehicle, a vegetable van, demolished the rail and a telegraph pole and rolled down the embankment to lie by our stern. The other blocked the bridge and had to be removed by a crane, but fortunately neither driver was hurt.

However, my carefree confidence was misplaced. We had properly arrived at Strasbourg as a coal barge in ballast, but when I had handed in the relevant papers at the customs office I found that we could not proceed to Colmar, where I wanted to see the Grünewald paintings in the Unterlinden museum, nor even out into the Rhine. We were now in the position of being aboard a yacht which was in France but had no papers of entry – and therefore could not have entered, as the customs officers in their smart launch pointed out with imperturbable French logic. And as we had not entered, we could not leave, *compris?*

Back home I recalled that Britain was one of the signatories to the Mannheim Convention of 1868 which followed upon the Treaty of Vienna and established a control over the navigation of the Rhine, and it was with hardly a hope that the government in Whitehall would know anything of Mannheim or its convention that I rang the Foreign Office and asked to be put through to the British representative on the Central Commission for the Navigation of the Rhine.

"Certainly, Sir," the operator astonished me. "Please hold the line a moment." And soon I was speaking to one of those charming, educated, mellifluous brigadiers who were filed away in poky offices in Whitehall as the Empire gradually contracted and collapsed, and who were kept there doing very little. From the difficulty I had in extricating myself from conversation with the gentleman responsible for Britain's theoretical presence on the Rhine I suspected it might have been the first time his telephone had ever been ringing. Indeed, he hinted as much and begged me to telephone him again, but when it came to discussing our problem he pointed out that we were still technically on the canal and not on the Rhine, so his mandate did not extend to cover us. All the same, he was ready to agree that French officials could be difficult. "Absolute blighters," he confided encouragingly. "The only way with the French is to keep hammering and hope."

The impasse was broken at last at the British Consulate in Strasbourg. When I put the matter to the lady vice-consul she rang a bell on her desk and ordered that Jacques should attend immediately. Jacques did so, wearing a boiler-suit and holding a spanner and an oily rag. He was chauffeur, handyman and boilerman to her Brittanic Majesty's outpost in Alsace, but he was also the mastermind behind its operations. He was, as the vice-consul explained, listed on the pay-roll as driver and concierge, but he was really employed because he was the only member of the staff who could predict infallibly the curious way in which the mind of the French civil service would work. Any diplomatic success, and one could be sure that the brain of Jacques was at the back of it, I gathered.

Jacques listened carefully to the tale of our difficulties, stared at the floor for a while, then suggested that it could be a case for the exercise of female charm. Failing that, Sanara. So the vice-consul willingly accompanied me to one office after another and exhaled charm and elegance over each official desk and counter in turn, only to receive impeccable courtesies but nothing else. By midday it was clear that charm was out and we must turn to Sanara.

Sanara lived a long way down a dock-side railway siding. In full the name meant the Alsatian Society for Navigation of the Rhine, and it was of course another anonymous society. A notice inside the door advertised the extraction of ships from customs as a speciality, and a clerk said that they would be only too willing to issue all the necessary papers for twelve thousand (old) francs. After a certain amount of bargaining I settled for two and a half thousand, the papers were issued, and an athletic lad was summoned to run all the way to the Strasbourg customs office to have them stamped. At last we were free, and the ability of Jacques and the wisdom of employing him were vindicated.

Nowadays any boat-owner can pass in or out of France with no more than minor formalities, a handshake, and a slight aroma of garlic. Even so, the Meuse is very little frequented, and with the diversion of most of the barges to the Moselle route the commercial traffic is a mere fraction of what it once was. Yet I doubt if any stretches of river can be more magnificent than the Meuse of the Ardennes with its course winding great loops between forest banks and cliffs of grey shale which in places rise a thousand feet above the stream. The woodland is impassable to all except deer and wild boar, and between Givet and Charleville each corner turned reveals a new stretch of astonishing grandeur. Villages there are, but they are neither interesting nor picturesque. It is the nature which is so arresting, all the way through the great forest to where the valley opens out at Charleville and the river becomes pastoral, but also one of tragic memories. For Sedan lies ahead and, a day's run beyond that, Verdun.

Nowadays the name of that town awakens only faint echoes. The slaughter in that beautiful valley is too remote in time, too incredible in its vastness to strike the imagination of the new generation. Schoolchildren and busloads of tourists on the way through to other destinations look casually at the statue of General Mangin, the 'Saviour of Verdun', standing very dapper and French in his cape and pillbox hat, and admire the fortified gateway, and perhaps buy a box of the sugared almonds for which the place is renowned. When first I drew in at Verdun's quayside there were groups of elderly men, often with berets and wearing a row of medals, walking through the streets and over the bridge. They were men from other lands, parties of British Legion men and their counterparts across the Atlantic, groups of former combatants from the French provinces. As young men all of them had known the horror of Verdun, and the heroism too. Now before they were too old to travel they had come back to the scene of comradeship and suffering. I found their presence very moving. They were the lucky ones who had come through that ordeal. Now they too are gone, the last survivors of a folly which was more drawn out than Hiroshima but vastly more destructive in that ten times as many were slaughtered in the battle of the Meuse.

That first time I voyaged up the river I was also struck by something very strange. It was midsummer, and in the thickets the nightingales were singing. The reed beds were a-twitter with the harsh rasping songs of the reed buntings and sedge warblers. A golden oriole flew across the canal, and the countryside was alive as it should have been. Then after locks 22 and 21 there came a sudden change. The marigolds and cuckoo-pint were there as before, but beyond the canal banks the chalky soil was a garden of wild thyme and scabious, butter-and-eggs and campanula. It was as though nature had felt forced to make its own memorial garden to those whose bones had been scattered over the rolling countryside. Yet not a bird sang along those reaches. I once wrote down that fact, and at a publisher's party of some kind in London a man came up to me and introduced himself as having been commissioned to write a history of the battle for Verdun. He had travelled along the valley, he said, and he had noticed that same fact. Some extraordinary oppressive weight of human guilt and folly hung over the meadows, and the woodlands planted to cover the scene of the worst of the carnage, and not a single birdsong broke the awful silence. He had wondered if he had imagined it, but now he knew he had not.

The conifers were planted because nothing could ever restore those summer meadows of the valley to what they had been. Not a blade of grass, not a flower or bush was left. Only the charred and blackened stumps of the largest of the trees projected fearfully from a landscape of craters and mud and human remnants when at last a halt was called to the killing.

Top: The author's first boat, *Commodore*, in Brinkebergskulle Lock on the Göta river.

Bottom: Thames Commodore, successor to *Commodore*, in a lock on the Canal du Midi.

A lock-keeper on the 'Left-Handed' canals.

The evil that men do lives after them, and I am sure that the spirit of senseless hatred and slaughter can somehow infect a place so that even the creatures are silent. And if this is so, one could expect it of the Meuse valley around Verdun as of hardly any other locality. To either side I could see the hills with their distant crests topped with monuments, British and French, Canadian and American, and here and there the geometric rows of graves. One hundred and sixty thousand bodies were recovered rotting on the slopes, in the dug-outs and trenches or buried in the debris of land-mines. And yet these were only a fraction of those who died around Verdun, the rest being so torn to pieces by shell and mortar that they could never be reassembled or even identified. These were the 'missing' – a gentle word to cover such horror. Their flesh was a feast for the carrion crows and the marsh harriers and kites whose descendants still hovered over the stream, though in the later stages of the battle even the birds of prey had their wings torn off and their feathers stripped by the incessant concussion of the artillery barrages, a pounding so intense that nine whole villages disappeared from the face of the earth, homes, houses and barns, church and all. After the war their former location was estimated by surveyors so that a signboard could be placed to show where the site of them had been.

Patiently, sadly, the bones of those who had gone as sheep to the slaughter or had heroically believed that they were dying for a better world were collected together and the giant ossuary of Douaumont was built to hold them, its forty-six huge vaults corresponding to the forty-six sectors of that incredible battle. Incredible, because surely one day a time must dawn when Verdun is still not entirely forgotten but has become a legend of a different kind, a time when humanity has reached a stage at which it is almost impossible to believe that the armies of the civilised world were once locked for month after month in such a struggle that more than a million men were shot, drowned in the river, bayoneted, buried alive in collapsing earthworks, or blown into unrecognisable tatters of blood and brain, bowels and rags, while nearly as many were taken home to their families blinded or crippled or shell-shocked, or to pass the rest of their lives demented in institutions.

★ ★ ★

The climb up the Meuse is gentle, the locks generally far apart – there are only fifty-eight in the hundred and seventy miles upstream of Givet – and many of them isolated, hidden away in the Ardennes forest, far from a farming hamlet or any other habitation at all. They are of course the small, hand-worked, one-barge-sized locks, each with its rather primitive house devoid of most main services where the keeper lives. The family usually has some sort of vegetable garden, and probably a few hens and maybe a couple of goats or even sheep, as well as cats and an amiable lock dog which begs lumps of sugar from any boat passing through. It was at one of these locks buried in the forest that I had a strange adventure spread over a number of years.

It was on my first voyage through the Ardennes that *Commodore* came round a long bend towards this particular lock and found the gates shut at either end. In the cut beyond the lock a laden barge was drifting slowly down waiting for the gates to be opened. But there was no sign of the lock-keeper.

The barge blew off several times on his loud hooter, but without result. No keeper appeared, so instead of hanging in the river to wait until the barge had come through I put *Commodore's* nose hard into the bank, jumped ashore with a line and then went up to the lock. There was nobody about, so I went to the upper gates and raised all four paddles to fill the lock for the barge. When I had done so I returned to the cottage and knocked on the door. There was no answer. Nor was there a dog. The only livestock were some rather dirty hens walking in and out of the open doorway.

Curiosity made me go inside and knock on an inner door, without result. I opened it. There on the stone floor was the lock-keeper, his head close to the ash-pan of the iron stove which was burning away fiercely. The man was dripping with sweat and his face was as red as that of a drunken Irishman. He looked to me to be under thirty, and I saw he was a stocky figure, robust and with rounded features. I knelt down and found he was panting. There was no smell of drink, so I shook him gently by the shoulder.

The man opened his eyes and put his hand on his forehead. I pulled him back from the stove, because I feared he might get heat stroke if he baked his head in the way he was doing. He then managed to struggle to his feet and I made him lie on the sofa while I opened the gates for the barge. I pulled a blanket over him and went out to wind away at the gate windlasses. The waiting barge chugged quietly into the lock and I explained to the skipper that he would have to look after the locking himself, as the lock-keeper was ill. Then I returned to the cottage.

It did not need much imagination to see that the man had a sharp attack of flu, and even if his shivering had drawn him to lie by a stove which was almost red hot he was obviously rather better placed on the sofa. He was reasonably alert, so I told him to wait where he was and I fetched some aspirin from *Commodore's* medicine chest and dosed him. The water did him good, and I had no worries about his passing a reasonable night, but at the same time I decided to take *Commodore* through the lock and bring her into the bank ahead and wait there until next day. The man was evidently all on his own, there was no telephone, and I wanted to make sure his sickness was nothing more serious. Besides, if he kept going out into the cold April wind every time a barge came it would not do him any good. In those days the Moselle had not been opened and the traffic from Lorraine to the Low Countries all passed by the Meuse, and there might be thirty or more ships in a day.

When he had cooled a little I took his temperature, which was still up around 102°. He had never seen this done before, and evidently regarded it as something like magic, because he later told a barge-skipper that an Anglais had a sort of stick he could put in ones mouth to show what was wrong. It may seem improbable that he could not know what a thermometer was, but of course the continental habit is to stick it up the anus, where the patient cannot see it and may not know precisely what is going on.

I began to take stock of the situation. The cottage was very run down, and dirty. The chicken manure on the stone tiles did not make it smell particularly attractive either. There was the remains of a simple meal on the table but no evidence of much cooking. The man was clearly living on his own in a condition which was by no means unusual in France, but in this case seemed depressing as though something was wrong. However, next morning he appeared at the lockside looking very much better. He was rubicund but not jovial. It seemed as though he were neither sad nor particularly happy, but there was nothing unusual in this either. He had very little voice, but I put this down to the natural effects of flu, so I gave him a supply of aspirins for two days and wrote down the exact times at which he was to take them. Then we set off again for Charleville and Strasbourg.

Two years later I again passed up the Meuse. It was a time of flooding and on one of the great loops of river there were more than thirty barges waiting because the lock ahead was under water and could not be worked. I walked up to ask the man in charge about the depth over the weir, and he assured me that there was a metre and a half. If I could make more speed than the flood pouring over the top there was no reason why I should not try to pass all the waiting craft and force a way over the top of the barrage.

Commodore was not a fast boat. Seven knots was as much as she could muster, but I worked her up on eddies, watched by an astonished and enthusiastic crowd of skippers and their families, and put the whole queue behind us. Next day we were up to the lock of the young man who had had the flu, and as his cottage came in sight the whole affair came back to me.

The cottage was even more run down than before. Weeds were growing unchecked against the walls and the hens had trampled the mud into the doorway. But the lock-keeper was there, red-faced and ill-shaved and morose. However, he recognised me and croaked in a half whisper that he had recovered completely soon after I had left on that earlier occasion. Yet his inability to speak worried me and I asked him what was the matter.

Nothing, he whispered somewhat gloomily. His voice had gone; slowly but surely it had left him. He was obviously trying to tell me this in ordinary speech but only a slight rasping sound came out.

I asked him if he had seen a doctor. Yes, indeed, the inspector had sent him to the doctor in the next town, who could make nothing of it. The doctor had referred him to a specialist at the county hospital at Charleville, and he had been taken in for observation and examination. They had done a number of tests, and had informed him that there was nothing they could do for him. He had lost his voice, and that was that. But it did not greatly matter, as he lived alone and had no one to talk to.

We worked the lock together, shook hands, and *Commodore* went on her way. The young man puzzled me greatly, and so did the medical diagnosis – or rather, the lack of one. The keeper was not a drinker, he was physically strong and sound, and yet there was something that did not quite fit. However, that was none of my business.

It was again a year or two before I steered *Commodore* up the Meuse once more, and coming round the familiar bend between the hills I wondered whether the red-faced young man would still be there. Indeed he was, and he waved a pleasant welcome as he opened the bottom gates to admit the boat. I glanced towards the cottage. It's whole appearance was one of neglect, and even despair.

I had the habit of tuning the radio in the saloon to France Musique, the French equivalent of Radio 3. It was playing away now, and the sound could be heard through the saloon windows. As the keeper walked along the lock-side to open the upper paddles and came level with the boat he paused, putting his head on one side.

"Bach's Brandenburg Concerto Number Two," he whispered. He said it almost inaudibly and yet as naturally as if he had been remarking that it was a fine day. It was such an unlikely remark to come from this individual, and the correct identification of the music so utterly improbable, that I let him listen till the music came to an end. Then we walked to the top of the lock and worked the paddles together. When the pen was full I told him I was going to stop above his lock, and would walk back. By now the Moselle navigation had opened, giving a faster and easier route to Rotterdam or Antwerp for craft coming from the Lorraine coal and steel area, and the Meuse was not the busy waterway it had been in earlier years. We were not likely to be disturbed.

So I made fast to the bank above the weir and went back to the lock-house. The keeper led me straight into his kitchen-parlour which smelt of hens and stale food. He gave me the wooden chair and sat on his creaky settee. Then he got up and made two mugs of coffee to pass the time while he was collecting himself. A few moments later the barrier collapsed, and his whole desperate sadness came gushing out in his strange croaking whisper.

As a boy he had been very fond of music. If ever there was a concert in his home town he would go to it, and as he had a good voice he sang in a local choir too. From school he was sent to a music teacher who trained him, because he intended to make a career in singing. He even hoped that one day he might reach the Paris opera. It happened that the county provided a small number of scholarships for advanced vocal training, and full of hope and with the encouragement of his teacher he entered the competition.

He failed.

He could not face his former classmates, the people down his street who knew he was bound for a singing career, his former teachers, even his parents. He left home, not knowing what to do, and in looking for work he found that the Bridges and Highways were in need of lock-keepers, so he applied. He asked for an appointment to somewhere far from his native town, far away from anywhere, so that he could bury his failure and be forgotten. They offered him this lock on the Meuse, and he took it. He had been there alone ever since. No, he had never gone home. He never went out to the village either. He never wrote to anyone. He had no contact with the outside world except for the passing barges.

One did not need to be a great detective to see why the man had lost his voice. It was as simple a case of psychosomatic illness as one could come across, and I was astonished that the specialists at the hospital had not investigated his past history. Perhaps they had, but shame at failure had led him to conceal the truth.

I stayed at the lock for an hour or two, and the conversation that took place between the two of us in hoarsely whispered French and my own halting attempts at the same language can be left to the imagination. Very likely the content did not greatly matter. The dam of guilt and failure had given way, and that was more important than anything else.

One day next summer my phone rang and a voice asked me if I was aware that it was Anglo-Belgian Cultural Relations Year. I admitted that I did not know that remarkable fact, but the speaker then went on to say that the Flemish Television had decided that nothing could be better than to mark it by a programme showing an English boat making its way up a Belgian river. They wanted *Thames Commodore* on the Meuse, and if I could bring the boat to Liege in two or three days ...

Here I had to interrupt and say that the journey from Agde on the Mediterranean to Liege would be more like three weeks hard flogging.

This was soon understood and we agreed that I should present myself with the boat and four suitably photogenic young people at Liege and be ready to cast off at nine o'clock on the morning of September 1st. During the intervening weeks I thought I had been foolish indeed to agree to anything of the kind, and when at Liege I saw the television crew arrive alongside I was convinced that it would be a dreadful experience. However, sartorial appearances can be very deceptive. We had a most agreeable time, and Paul Jambers the director or producer (I can never remember which is which) won a prize with the film at the Cannes Festival.

Although we were supposed to be filming in Belgium, Jambers got carried away with the scenic beauty of the Meuse and he decided to beg some extra days and reels of film and shoot the French river too, right up to Charleville. Thus it was that once again I came in sight of the lock with the failed vocalist. I purposely said nothing to the television crew about what had happened in the past, as I feared that the wrong kind of interest might be shown.

This time there was a surprise. The cottage had been white-washed, the window-frames and door painted. The hens were in a wire enclosure with a proper henhouse, and red roses were climbing gaily up the wall of the house. There was a neat patch of vegetables too at one side. But the man who stood by the gate to wind it shut after we had moved in was not the red-faced keeper I had come to know so well. For a moment I thought there had been a change, but then I recognised the thin, angular man in a cap as the *remplacant,* the spare man who stood in at each of six locks in succession to work it during the free day of the resident keeper.

I asked him if the regular keeper was the same as before. Yes indeed, the stand-in replied. Only he was not there at the moment. He had driven into Charleville to do the shopping. But if I would like to speak madame ...

Madame! So the shyness and self-effacement had been conquered to such an extent that my friend had actually got married. It was no wonder that everything looked so neat and orderly.

I knocked at the door, and a young woman came out who radiated happiness, and competence too. We talked for a few moments and I admired her flowers, and the vegetable patch. Then I took my leave.

"Tell your husband that the Anglais with the blue boat came through, Madame," I said. Then we moved on up the river to resume our filming. We had to find a place where *Thames Commodore* could be shot from a distance for a whole minute, to give a background for the credit titles.

Once again two years passed before I was on my way to Southern France, passing as usual up the Meuse. I wondered what the state of affairs would be at the lock-house I had come to know so well, and as we came round the familiar bend I could see the stocky figure of the lock-keeper bending over the flower-bed. I blew off on the hooter and he looked round, strode to the bullnose at the lower end of the lock and hailed me welcome in a voice that would have done justice to a town crier.

When the boat had risen, I stepped off and shook hands. Not a word was said about earlier times. The man was exuberant, clean and healthy, and when his wife came to the door I could see in his glance how he adored her.

"Bring the little one!" He wanted her to fetch the baby and show it to Ingrid. It was a lovely child, a little girl. We admired the baby with something very much more than mere polite interest. She was a wonderful ending to an unusual tale.

V

Adventures in the Lowlands

Ostend was only one of twenty or more entrances spread along the western coast of Europe and leading into a maze of waterways which evidently extended for hundreds of miles in every direction. As soon as I had experienced the ease of the broad waterways of Holland and the route which twisted and turned through the ancient Flemish cities to reach the Meuse, I wanted more. Waterways on the brain was a disease that was becoming chronic and incurable for the simple reason that another canal or river was always hiding round the next corner and begging to be explored. And another, and then another. But there was a frustrating limit in the form of a mathematical formula constructed of locks and miles and river currents on the one hand and the length of the school summer holidays on the other. Beyond that limit one could not stray. There was not the time available, especially when one had prudently kept three or four days in hand at either end against the possibility of being stuck in Ramsgate or Calais because of a storm in the Channel. However enticing the waterways might be which lay hidden further ahead, they had to be left unvisited.

The obvious solution was to forgo week-end voyaging on the Thames, at least during the summer months. That meant that one could run *Commodore* abroad in the spring and return by train and ferry having left her in some distant inland harbour until the summer holidays. Even better was to base her entirely abroad, and when on a summer's evening in 1955 she dropped down through Tower Bridge on her way to Dunkirk she was never to see the Thames again. Her new base was soon established at a yard on one of the smaller waterways leading out of the Lake of de Kaag in southern Holland. It was easily accessible from Amsterdam or the Hook of Holland, and it gave *Commodore* a flying start in April or midsummer, increasing the radius of her explorations by several hundred miles. But she had only been there for one winter when she set out on a voyage that was to keep her away for three years and add four more countries to her acquaintance. I had decided to head her for Scandinavia.

The canal route crossed Holland. I knew that this part of the voyage was easy, because I had already been as far as the Frisian lakes, fringed with low-eaved Frisian farms surrounded by wide Frisian fields grazed by the immaculate black and white Frisian cows which regarded passing craft with an expressionless Frisian stare. The route was used by two-thousand-tonners, and held no problems or terrors. After a day with Rembrandt in Amsterdam I thought it would be a pleasant change to leave the city in the dark and spend the night in the harbour of Marken, which was then an island in the continually shrinking Ijsselmeer, or Zuyderzee. This would be no problem either. I had been there several times already, and the reason for going at night was really a very sound one. Marken was a favourite with tourists, who began to arrive in their hundreds about nine or ten in the morning and filled the village until six in the evening. During those business hours the Markenaars were a hard-faced lot, the women standing in their doorways dressed up like dolls and the men ostentatiously sitting on the quay and appearing to mend nets. "We take dollars" was then the extent of their English, and provided one paid in ready cash they would be delighted to have their pictures taken or to show a visitor the knicknacks in their parlours. But with the departure of the last boat of the day the Markenaars relaxed. The racks of postcards were taken in, the men put away their clay pipes and lit cigarettes, the women took off their bonnets and stood around gossiping like humans. Marken became in an instant a pleasant little place where the inhabitants would stop by our hatch to chat and laugh without payment. Out of hours I liked the place.

We had on board a friend who was soon to suffer so badly from waterways on the brain that he wrote a couple of books about travels on English canals, and became a stalwart of the Inland Waterways Association too. Fred Doerflinger and his wife were accompanying us as far as we would run in a fortnight.

Now I knew very well that the Dutch engineers were continually taking bites out of the Ijsselmeer to turn it into land, and also that they intended to join Marken to the mainland and – alas – give it a main road access and a giant carpark. So it was reasonable for me to spend a few guilders on a new and up-to-date chart of the Ijsselmeer, and this I did. It was corrected up to a date six weeks before we set out from the city docks on a clear summer's night and left Amsterdam behind us.

And a very lovely night it was too, still and with the faintest touch of haze. I ran out far enough to clear the eel nets which extended some distance from the shore, then set a course for Marken. After an hour or so we had its lighthouse ahead, and I sat leaning back against the windshield while Fred was at the wheel beside me. Naturally he was facing forward, but I was seated looking the other way, thinking how very graciously the new moon shone upon our wake astern, its light sparkling off the wavelets at the edge of our wash. I have always liked a voyage in the night, and on this occasion the conditions were ideal. It was calm, we could see our destination marked by its light. The air was still and just pleasantly cool, and the night was not so dark that we could run down stakes or obstructions.

I forget what we were talking of, Fred and myself, when at exactly ten minutes past eleven he made a curious remark.

"Funny what a shadow that cloud makes just ahead," he said. "It looks like a great sort of pipe".

I happened to be looking toward the moon and could see that there was no cloud to make a shadow of any kind. I did not even turn to look ahead before pushing the gear lever into astern and forcing the accelerator right back. The water foamed out from under the stern, and the momentum was taken off the ship to such an extent that when she struck the new Marken dike a few seconds later she was only making about two thirds her humble speed of six knots. A dark shape rose up in the moonlight. It was a startled cow.

I had often discussed with experienced ancient mariners the procedure to be followed in the event of any accidental stranding or breakdown at sea. Nowadays it is fashionable for yachtsmen to exhibit the name of their boat in letters two feet high on canvas wind-shields on either side, but it had been impressed upon me that if one had reasonable hopes of being able to deal with the emergency unaided, then the first thing to be done was to remove the ensign and any tell-tale burgees, and swiftly to paint out the name of the vessel and port of registry. If accosted and addressed one should assume that salvage money dominated the mind of the inter-vener and decline to understand English or any other known language except Greek if in the north, or Finnish if in southern waters. Part of the object was of course to avoid clever locals from holding one up for a ransom of salvage money, but another was to prevent news from reaching the underwriters, kindly men who could easily take fright unnecessarily and wonder whether they might have to postpone for a week or two the purchase of their new Rolls Royces.

By good fortune I was spared the painting out, because it was at night that we had landed among Marken's cattle and all I needed to do was to turn off the main electric switch at once and let the boat be swallowed up in darkness. The good people of Marken were evidently early bedders, for there was not a lighted window to be seen in the village. We were not likely to be disturbed.

The next thing was for me to put on bathing pants and jump overboard into water that was pleasantly warm. I took a flashlamp and examined *Commodore's* hull, which I soon found had not even received a scratch on the paintwork. She had a solid iron keel, shallow but broad, and this had ridden up a flat boulder so that I could see right under her from side to side near the bow, while the stern was correspondingly tilted down so that the water was several inches over the boot-topping, the paint line normally three or four inches over the surface.

I had to do a lot of under-water landscape gardening to remove all the stones and lumps of basalt which might hit her screw or belly when she came off, but rocks being appreciably lighter in water than in air this was surprisingly easy. However, she was too solidly aground to come off under the modest power of her engine, so the next thing was to let out all the water from her tank and to move from the hold in the bow ten sacks of coke – for she had an open stove for cold nights – and any other movable weights, piling them on the stern. From time to time Fred tried to wriggle her hard astern, but it was no use. I was beginning to think she was destined to become a rubbing post for cows unless we paid a fishing boat to drag us off in the morning.

After three hours a breeze got up, blowing on to the dyke. The waves made her lollop a little so I had to row two anchors out far astern to prevent her being nudged on her hind end and pushed even harder ashore. All the while not a sound came from the houses nearby, and I was determined to get off the dyke before the fishermen started out soon after dawn, as they usually did.

I walked along the dyke top into the village to see if any useful gear might be lying about. At one of the cattle gates I found the post against which the gate closed somewhat loose. It was a mighty oaken post, and it might have been specially designed as a lever for thirteen-ton admiral's barges. I worked it to and fro until it could be drawn like a bad tooth, and then hauled it back along the dyke-top to the scene of the stranding. In the water I built up a pile of rocks as a fulcrum and stuck the end of the lever under the keel. Fred hung the dinghy on a long slack line and I stationed it close to me. Then I told him to start up and put the ship full speed astern. As he did so I took a jump on to the end of the lever. *Commodore's* bow jumped up, and she then shot backwards so fast that I only just managed to grab the transom of the dinghy with one hand as it fled from the dyke.

We had been five hours and twenty minutes on the rocks, and when the first of the Markenaars strolled down to the harbour we were lying peacefully alongside their quay, the coke sacks were in the hold, the gate-post had been carried back to the village and installed again so firmly that none could have told that it had ever been moved, and a pleasant smell of coffee was drifting up from the galley to mix with the tang of fish which always seemed to hang over the island.

★ ★ ★

Three days later the tide of the Ems estuary was carrying us up past Emden, heading for the Küsten Canal, the waterway link from the Ems to the Weser. It was nearly supper time when we came up to a broad cut which led off to the side, and as it looked enticing I turned into it. Passing through a large harbour lock we found ourselves mooring in front of the townhall of a place I had never heard of, the town of Leer. As I jumped down with the lines the thud startled a woman in a small barge of firewood lying at the jetty. She put her head out of the hatch, and was so astonished at the sight of *Commodore's* ensign that she gasped a "Himmeldonner-wetternocheinmal," and that was all that she could think of to say for the moment. But next morning she explained in detail that we need not proceed further up the Ems. We could cut the corner. From Leer a river led to the Elisabethfehn Canal which cut across the moors to meet the main barge route half way along its course. It would save us forty kilometres and several hours. She had been through it herself more than once. Nothing could be simpler, she said.

Without her advice I would never have found the Elisabethfehn Canal, and it was hard enough to discover it even with her detailed directions. We passed under a tide gate and soon found ourselves in a waste of moors in which the channel continually forked and the course eventually petered out. The only native I could find in this wilderness was a lad who could neither speak German nor be certain which was the right way to the entrance of the canal, but when we came to a bascule bridge with electric winding gear I knew we must at last have struck the correct route. When once in the canal itself we came to a railway bridge which was just being closed. Trains were rare on this line, but even so the bridge could not be opened again before five o'clock in the evening. When I saw how the bridge operated I could appreciate that a gap of at least two hours between trains was needed if the bridge were to be opened and then closed again. The track of the short section over the water was mounted on a pontoon tank, and to raise the rails clear of the abutments on which they rested water had to be pumped out of the tank with a small pump and a two-stroke motor-mower engine. After that the span could be wound out of the gap with windlasses and cables. The closure was an equally lengthy business but at last we reached the Küsten Canal near Ahrensdorf in pouring rain and darkness somewhat after ten o'clock at night, about seven hours later than if we had taken the longer route. But I did not mind. I had had the experience of the railway bridge and could admire the ingenuity of the unknown heroes of the Royal Engineers who had thought it up ten years earlier. Besides, the delay was to bring the opportunity of a strange meeting.

Shortly after six in the morning I was awakened by a thumping on the side of the boat, near my head. I looked up and saw a round, ruddy face pressed against the glass of the window. Its owner was a young man of

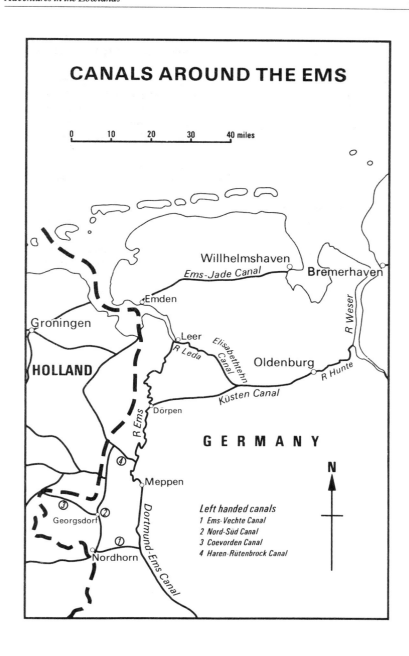

CANALS AROUND THE EMS

0 10 20 30 40 miles

Willhelmshaven

Ems-Jade Canal

Bremerhaven

Emden

R Weser

Groningen

Leer

R Leda

Elisabethfehn Canal

Oldenburg

R Hunte

HOLLAND

Küsten Canal

Dörpen

R Ems

GERMANY

N

④

Meppen

③

Georgsdorf

②

Dortmund-Ems Canal

①

Nordhorn

Left handed canals
1 Ems-Vechte Canal
2 Nord-Süd Canal
3 Coevorden Canal
4 Haren-Rütenbrock Canal

about thirty-five who stood there in his shirt sleeves in the pouring rain, beaming in through the window like a rising sun. He had seen the mast above the bank and so he had come to invite us home to breakfast, he explained. His name, he said, was Kruse, Hans Kruse.

Over the top of the bank he led us to the only house within sight. It was an inn which stood lonely and windswept on a slight rise of the soggy moorland. There was no road, but a rough track led to the inn across the marshy land. Naturally enough there were no other customers when we trailed in so early in the morning. I wondered that he had any at other times but he assured us that peat cutters and weekend fishermen dropped in for a glass of beer or a schnaps, or even a meal. I had never been able to understand the economics of German country pubs, but they seemed to be able to survive in a simple way on a minimum of trade with a bit of smallholding and a few domestic animals.

It was still early enough for the rest of the household to be either asleep or behind the scenes in the kitchen, but the fact that our host was married was obvious from the fact that the saloon was tidy and clean even at that early hour in the morning. There was a sort of bar in the corner and we sat on stools along one side of it with our jovial friend on the other. He did not ask what we wanted for breakfast, but poured it out. Brandy.

Soon his wife came in for a moment, probably from curiosity, and so did his son who was getting ready to leave for school, though where that could be I could not imagine. His proud father insisted that he spoke a few words to us in English, which he did. Then he took his satchel and disappeared into the rain.

We drank our brandy, expressed our thanks and were ready to leave. But the brandy proved only to be a starter. There was another species of brandy to come, and as time passed a third and then a fourth, after which Kruse thought a cup of coffee was called for. His wife brought it in with a macaroon, there being apparently no bread left in the house. It was an unusual start to the day, and all the while Kruse was beaming and sipping his brandy and saying how astonishing it was to see a British boat on the Küsten Canal and asking me where I was heading, although like most people I met in Lower Saxony his geographical knowledge had a limit within a radius of not much more than twenty miles.

At the end of this hospitable breakfasting Kruse asked if I would do something for him. I had no idea what it might be, but I had no wish to appear ungrateful. Besides after such a breakfast I was ready to wrestle with principalities and powers and even spiritual wickedness in high places.

Kruse then produced from the liqueur cupboard a bottle of juniper gin and stood it on the counter. Could I oblige him by taking the bottle to England and giving it to the farmer at the farm with the white gate?

I said I would endeavour so to do if he could tell me where the farm was. He replied that it was in Uxbridge.

Now Uxbridge had never struck me as farming country, and I said so. But Kruse was certain that Uxbridge was the correct place. He could not recall the name of the farmer and was not sure that he had ever known it. But could I not find the farm? There would not be so many farms in Uxbridge would there? Especially with a white gate.

I reminded myself that Kruse had also had four kinds of brandy, and double measures too, but there was something so appealing about his extraordinary request that I undertook to find the farm and personally to deliver the goods. It would not be much more than half an hour's drive to Uxbridge from Highgate. But I was curious to know how he had an acquaintance in London's outer suburbia, and yet did not know his name or address.

Kruse then unfolded the tale that lay behind his asking. He had been drafted into the army and was lucky enough to be taken prisoner by the British. At the end of the war he was shipped over to a camp in England, and from there he was taken out in the mornings by lorry to work on a farm, and fetched in the evenings. He was the only one let out to this particular farm at Uxbridge, and he loved every moment of his time there. For several months he worked as a cowherd, an occupation which was very much in his line, for his own parents had kept a few head of cattle here in the moors. It was not like being a prisoner, not at all. The food in the camp was infinitely better than anything he would have had in Germany in those dark days just after the war, but best of all was the extraordinary kindness he had from the farmer, who treated him as a son.

Time went by in this happy way, he said, and always he had wanted to be able to say to the farmer how grateful he was. Perhaps he was shy, or he could not find the words in a strange tongue. And then one morning the warrant officer at the camp had told him to be ready earlier than usual. The truck was taking him, not to the farm, but on the first stage of his repatriation. He was going home – and he had not even the chance to say goodbye to his friend the farmer.

I asked Kruse how old he thought the farmer was. Over sixty, he replied. I added ten years for the intervening time and wondered to myself whether the man would still be alive, but I promised to take the bottle of East Frisian liquor to the farm as soon as I was home again.

Just as we were preparing to leave the inn two things occurred to me. First, there was every chance that I would not be able to trace the farm if all I knew was that it had a white gate and was against all probability stated to be in Uxbridge. If I could not deliver the goods, Kruse might well think I had decided to keep the liquor myself, so I would have to deliver it, come what might. A snag on the other side was that if I turned up at a farm with this splendid gift and asked if they remembered a young

German who had worked there ten years earlier the answer might very well be "Yes, of course. Thanks very much". To cover this last eventuality I ran back to the boat for my camera and took a simple passport-style head-and-shoulders photograph of Kruse. Then we took our leave.

Two weeks later we were back in Highgate, and on the following Sunday afternoon drove out with the Doerflingers to Uxbridge. Farms there might well have been a century or two ago, but not a mere ten years back, I felt sure. When I went into the police station and asked with apparent confidence to be directed to the farm with a white gate, I was courteously informed by a helpful sergeant that I must have got the name of the locality wrong. Uxbridge was not a farming area, he pointed out. It was light industrial. He could absolutely assure me that there were no farms dotted about the place with or without white gates.

We had brought with us an Ordnance Survey map, and now we began to describe rough semi-circles on the side of Uxbridge away from the metropolis, following all the by-roads and asking at any farm whether they knew of one with a white gate – and incidentally if their own gate looked comparatively new enquiring whether they had changed it in the last ten years. We covered the ground from Uxbridge to Rickmansworth and Ruislip, then further out as far as near to Slough and up to the Chalfonts, but there were no white gates even if there were farms by the dozen. Their owners were anxious to help, but none could think of any farm to suit our description until near Gerrards Cross a man who was trimming a hedge said promptly "Ah, you'll be meaning Mr Field's. White Gate Farm, that's what they calls it." And he gave us directions to find it.

This farm was not within ten miles of Uxbridge, but the explanation was simple. The prisoner-of-war depot had certainly been at Uxbridge, and it was from there that Kruse and others went out every day to be dumped at their respective places of work at various points all over Buckinghamshire. To them the whole area was part of the arrangements of the camp at Uxbridge.

A driveway led up an avenue of young trees to the farmhouse and outbuildings. The cowhouse was on the right. The door was open, and inside I could see a thin, white-haired and slightly bent elderly man gently stroking the shoulders of a cow and talking to her as he did so. That, I was sure, was the man I was seeking. I produced the photograph and asked Mr Field to look at it.

"Why, that's Hans the cowman," he exclaimed. And then, anxiously, "There's nothing happened to him, has there?"

I reassured him. No, Hans Kruse was in excellent health, I said, and I explained how I had met him in his remote inn on the moors of Lower Saxony. Then I told how sad Kruse had been to be taken away without so much as a chance to thank Mr Field for his great kindness.

The farmer was greatly moved. "Hans, he was a fine lad", he said. "None of my men ever cared for the cattle the way he did. I took a great liking to him. He was like a son to me. And then one day they just took him off and I never heard of him again. I didn't even know where they sent him, not even what part of Germany he lived in, and time and time over I thought to myself why on earth had I not asked him before it was too late. Then I could have had him come back and stay with us for his holidays. We could have gone to the Windsor horse show together. He would have liked that, Hans would. And this foolishnesss, our own lads and good fellows like Hans being made to fight each other – it is madness, isn't it? Madness ...."

Tears came into his eyes when I unwrapped the bottle of spirits. Mr Field could only speak with difficulty.

"And just to think that after all these years Hans should think of me. But now that you can tell me where he lives I'll write to him myself. Do you think he could understand it if I did?"

I told Mr Field that Kruse's son learned English at school and already spoke it tolerably well.

"Then I'll write tonight. And I'll have him over for the next horse show at Windsor. That is, if I'm spared".

I never saw Kruse again, and because the Küsten Canal ran between two very high banks I never managed to identify the position of our mooring on that wet and windy night.

* * *

On my next journey that way I was returning from Scandinavia, and I decided that it would be wiser not to take the Elisabethfehn route but to follow the Küsten Canal to its end and turn left into the river Ems, run up it for sixty miles or so and then try my hand at the Left-Handed Canals, which should provide a shorter way to pass into Holland and eventually reach our base south of Amsterdam. These canals were left-handed in name because they were described as *Linksemsisch*, or on the left hand of the Ems, and instead of belonging to the state they were the property of an entity called the *Genossenschaft der Linksemsischen Känale*, which took the dues at a toll house at the entry to the system, where the Ems-Vechte Canal joined the Ems.

The canal was a small one, and it ran straight as a die across the heathland between a double line of fir trees. After ten miles or so it entered the little town of Nordhorn where another canal turned off northward and the Ems-Vechte made a circuit of the town before aiming westward. Not far beyond the town we came to a somewhat simple lock at Frensdorferhaar, a hamlet which appeared to consist of a farm by the lock and a low building on the opposite side, standing back among a group of trees. On a tree by the farm gate a faded notice bore the message *Deutsch-Niederländische Grenze. Übertritt Verboten.* One end of the lock appeared to be in Germany, the other in Holland. But there was nobody about, neither customs-man nor passport control officer. There was no fence, no barrier. It seemed surprisingly un-Germanic.

I was wondering how to set about the locking when a man came out into the farmyard carrying a pail of milk. He stared at the boat, scratched his head, and then said he couldn't say by rights what ought to be done. No boat had been through Frensdorferhaar for more than a year, and a week later the canal was to be closed down. Yes, there were windlasses somewhere in the barn, he thought. The lock would probably work, but of course he must have authority to let us use the windlasses. After all, this was an international frontier, and what was more we were a foreign boat coming from yet another land, Sweden. It raised problems which were too great for him to contemplate. Perhaps we should enquire over there, he said, pointing at the red-roofed building across the canal. I walked over the lock-bridge and up to the house, and knocked on the door. It was in this way that I met Arno Piechoroswki.

Outside the door a blue canvas canoe was standing on end. I believe Arno had built it himself, and aboard this frail craft he had succeeded in doing something from which I had always been debarred by bad weather. The Bandak-Norsjö or Telemark Canal is one of the only two inland waterways in Norway, and in 1957 I worked *Commodore* to within thirty miles of its entrance, only to have to shelter for several days in a rock-strewn inlet of the Norwegian coast. By the time the storm died away there was not sufficient time left to voyage into the middle of the country. The next time I had reached the Kattegat when the weather broke and I had to decide whether or not to go further ahead. I chose not to, and as the stormy weather up in the Skagerrak continued for three weeks the decision proved sensible if disappointing. But Arno had really been there, so he was a real canal explorer. Of course he had not paddled all the way from Frensdorferhaar but had taken his canoe to Norway by train. All the same, he had been down the whole length of that improbable waterway, and I never met another who had done so.

Arno was headmaster of Frensdorferhaar school, which was the building with the red roof. He was deputy headmaster too, and bursar. He was also assistant bursar and head of the languages department, chief mathematician and all the rest of the staff. For the school at Frensdorferhaar was one of those rare and excellent institutions, a single teacher school. There were eight classes all in one room, except that Class 8 had as yet no pupils, none of the children having quite reached that eminence. The seven lower classes all had their approximate geographical limits in the one room, rather as robins have their definite but unmarked territorial lines in the garden. Arno would move from one to the other and teach them all in rotation. It was one great happy family, and Arno took me on a tour of the classes while we awaited the arrival of the astonished customs officers summoned by telephone from Nordhorn to perform the unlikely task of clearing a British ship which had arrived from Stockholm and was bound for the land on the other side of the notice-board nailed to the tree, via the Almelo-Nordhorn Canal, which began at the lock.

The formalities took some time because the officers wanted to make the most of the occasion, for within a week the canal was to be laid to rest. They also wanted cups of tea. Besides, the farmer had to find the windlasses, and then in his capacity as part-time *Schleusenmeister* to strain away at the creaking machinery until the gates could be opened and we could be duly seen to have left the Federal Republic. Meanwhile it was time for assembly and first lesson, and Arno was occupied in teaching. One class was learning Dutch, another curiously enough was having German lessons because, as he explained, the native language in this out-of-the-way corner of the Bundesrepublik was Saxon. Arno was also something of a poet, and in later years he sent me a book of his poems in Saxon, of which I could make neither head nor tail.

When it was time for break, Arno led the whole school down to the lock, and I told the children everything they wanted to know about England, and Sweden, and the Baltic and *Commodore*. Then as we left, they stood ranged across the bridge and sang us a lovely romantic song, *"Ach Bootsmann, wann fahren wir auf See?"* It was so perfect, so natural that I could not keep back the tears as I steered slowly away from them down the Dutch section of the canal toward Almelo.

This Dutch town was about twenty miles down the cut, and so weeded was the waterway that we had at times to resort to hauling from the bank. But we kept going, and in just over ten hours a massive steel bascule-bridge came in sight, which carried one of the main streets of Almelo over the Canal. The signal lights were at red but I could soon see that the keeper was not there. Nor was he nearby, and as nobody crossing the bridge had a notion of where he was to be found I hailed the offices of a bank and asked one of the girls to be so very kind as to telephone the police and ask for their assistance.

Very soon the Dutch police arrived and began to explain most apologetically that they had no key to the machinery. Only the bridge man had these, and for some unaccountable reason he was not there in his cabin. However, they undertook to find him, and for a long while we could hear the loud-speaker car roaming through the town calling for the bridge-keeper. It took them a long time to discover his whereabouts because they drew a blank until one of the officers had the idea that he might be in the cinema. They interrupted the performance to summon him to open up his bridge.

I felt sorry for the bridge man. For perhaps a year he had sat at the controls of his mighty bridge and never a boat had come in sight. One day he decided at last to sneak off to enjoy himself in the cinema, and of course it was bad luck that it was on that same afternoon that *Commodore* came up the cut. He was brought back to work in the police car, but at least he had the satisfaction of a grand and appreciative audience, because by this time most of Almelo was lining the canal banks to see the great sight of a real boat passing.

That was my first experience of the Left-Handed Canals, but it was not the last of my acquaintance with Arno, for we wrote to each other for many years, and I stayed with him and his wife Edda in their school-house, not at Frensdorferhaar but after they had moved. The move took place several years after our first meeting, and it happened against their will.

The German government wanted to make a study of how an ordinary small town could have changed – as they did in the Hitler period – from a place where everyone lived together in peace and harmony to one in which eventually the Jewish citizens and their families were ostracised, rejected, attacked, and finally rounded up and sent to their death. It was to some extent an enlightened idea to set up such an investigation, even if the reason was perhaps mainly a feeling of national guilt and a desire somehow to expiate or at least understand something of the awful crimes in which the nation had been involved. Whatever the reasons the decision was taken in Bonn, and a suitable community for the study had to be selected. The lot fell upon Nordhorn.

Arno Piechorowski had arrived after the war and came originally from Eastern Germany, so he had no local connections, no relatives in Lower Saxony. He had been in the Nordhorn area for some years already and knew his way about, but he could not be expected to have friends who were implicated, or to try to hush up unpleasant discoveries. He received a letter telling him that he had been given the special assignment of investigating the fate of the Jewish community in Nordhorn. He declined, telling the education authority that it was madness, and that if a dog was buried it had better stay buried. He would prefer to dedicate his life to his happy family in his school at Frensdorferhaar. Nothing was to be gained by raking up the past, he thought. It was the future that mattered.

Unfortunately Germany was not a land in which the civil service (which included school teachers) might choose what it preferred to do. Arno was courteously but firmly informed that the permission of his state education authority had been obtained, and he was assigned to the enquiry. He had better agree to it and get started. Again he protested that the authority in Lower Saxony might not be pleased to read the report when it came, but it was useless. He was given two years to do the work, so far as I recall, and he was authorised to ask questions of anyone he wished.

At the end of the two years Arno sent me a copy of his report. As he had foretold, there were almost none in Nordhorn who could show clean hands. The whole awful story was carefully set out, from the first notices posted on shop windows "Jewish Concern", to the occasional broken window, the refusal of entry to clubs, the allegations of eating too large a lunch on "self-denial days", the turning of a blind eye by the police, the indifference of the councillors and mayor. Arno described in horrifying simplicity the funeral of one of the town's most stalwart and loved Jewish members. Everyone knew and respected the man, and yet when he died only two old men out of the whole population had the bravery to walk bare-headed behind his coffin.

I could hardly bear to read further, but I did. Little by little the darkness closed in upon those ordinary members of the small town community who happened to be Jewish. When the last little group of them were escorted by the Nazis to the train that was to take them to their death none raised a finger, or a word of protest. But their businesses, their homes and property, their humble belongings – well, that was different.

The government was pledged to publish the report, and did so. But they could see as well as could Arno that after its publication he could not possibly stay in his beloved Frensdorferhaar. Too many of the guilty ones were still alive and in positions of respect. He was transferred to Baden-Württemberg, which found another school for the Piechorowskis, buried in the depths of the Black Forest and about as far in distance from Nordhorn as was possible.

Arno and Edda had already moved before I once again came to a halt at the stop-lock leading out of the Ems into the system of the Left-Handed Canals. The route to Almelo was certainly closed, but at Nordhorn we could turn right into the Nord-Süd Canal and head for a further canal junction at Georgsdorf, where we would pick up yet another Left-Handed waterway, the Coevorden-Piccardie Canal. Coevorden was in Holland and by this means I intended to reach *Commodore's* base south of Amsterdam.

Although we met no boat of any kind beyond Nordhorn the few simple little locks worked well enough and rather to my surprise each of them had an aged man or an old woman in charge of it and living in the lock cottage. All the locks were staffed until we came to the fourth, where no amount of hooting, shouting or knocking on the door produced any response. Of course there were no windlass handles either, but it was not for nothing that I had been through the K and A. I had my own handles aboard, and if they did not fit the spindles I was able to apply a heavy adjustable wrench instead, which was what I now did. To work the lock was not very difficult, but it happened to be crossed at one end by a minor road on a swing-bridge. After my experiences in Sweden (which I shall recall in a later chapter) and on the K and A, I was not particularly deterred by a bridge, even if it had not recently been used, and as this one had chains and warning discs to hang over the approaches on either side, I dutifully put them in place to stop the hypothetical traffic, swung the bridge, put everything back in order again, and was just starting off from the lock when a woman came out of the lock-house in a condition bordering on hysteria. How dared we operate the lock! And swing a bridge on a departmental road!! And not even show our ticket!!! I feared that if given the chance of a discussion she might have a seizure, so I called her the number on our ticket and waved her a pleasant farewell. Shouts drifted along the canal of how she would fetch the police, something which amused me somewhat as the chance of raising a policeman of any kind in this utterly deserted landscape was patently ridiculous.

An hour ahead we reached Georgsdorf, where there was another bridge, this time carrying a road that became the main street of the village. The regulation three long blasts did not cause the bridge to open, but brought two men in handsome black uniforms to step out of a smart car parked at the approach. Two more rather grey-looking men in macintoshes emerged from another car, and I rightly guessed that these were Left-Handed inspectors.

I was pleasantly surprised to see that the police were not just policemen but real, proper, correctly dressed water police such as one might find on the Dortmund-Ems Canal or the Rhine. Where they could have come from I never discovered, but they must have driven at least forty miles across country to catch us there at Georgsdorf. My reason for pleasure was that I knew the *Wasserschutzpolizei* to be sensible men, usually more interested in boats and waterways than in regimenting people in accordance with regulations.

As I climbed on to the bridge in the drizzle one of them gave me a hand over the rail. They then shook hands, ignored the two inspectors and started chatting amiably about our voyage. They admired *Commodore* and asked all about her engine, then about other trips we had made. The inspectors seemed continually to be on the point of butting in but they had no chance to interrupt the courtesies. At length one of the officers remarked in a casual fashion that some sort of complaint had been made about my not having shown the receipt for the dues to pass through the canal. I now showed it, and he nodded.

"And he worked the lock himself," the taller inspector managed to put in.

"And swung a road-bridge," added the smaller one indignantly.

"On a Departmental Road of Category One!"

"Yes. And to think of it. A bus could have run into the lock. A Category One Departmental Highway – why, it was dangerous in the extreme. If a bus ...."

I said there was no bus, the barriers were across the road, and if some madman in a bus had driven through them he could equally well have done it when the old lady had opened the bridge instead of me.

"But what would have happened if there *had* been a bus," piped the short inspector. "Yes, and it had run into the lock. What would have happened? Tell me that!"

"A large splash," I said.

The police officers laughed.

"I expect you wish to be on your way," said one of them with a smile.

I thanked him, and shook hands with them both.

"And everybody drowned! Whose fault would that have been do you think?" It was the taller inspector's turn, but by now I was climbing over the parapet to land on the deck. The police signed to the bridge man to drop the barriers and get ready to swing the bridge.

"There might have been twenty killed," the one inspector declaimed indignantly.

"Even more," agreed the other.

But the water police had deaf ears for their grumblings, and as the span was swung aside they saluted pleasantly and wished us all a successful voyage. I turned out of the Nord-Süd into the last link of the Left-Handed route.

The next fifteen miles of deserted and marshy land appeared to be inhabited by beasts which in the distance resembled the extinct *Stegosaurus*, huge creatures with massive heads bowing and raising themselves again as they dipped to pick up lesser animals and herbage. When seen closer they turned out to be specimens of a small well-head pump for oil, for we were now in an oilfield which seemed to look after itself. Our German map described the area briefly as 'desert'. The canal went straight across it, but at the further side of the wasteland the water broadened out ahead and had properly regulated stone-clad banks, a sure sign that we were about to cross into Holland. Just before this broadening was a rusty swing-bridge and beside it a notice, *Zoll*! On the bank stood a wooden hut in which sat a pleasant middle-aged man in green uniform. He was reading a novel, and the improbable sound of a motor had made him look up. Pulling on his smart peaked cap he signed to me to stop, and came aboard and looked at passports. Then he went ashore again, to return with the indispensable tools of his trade, a stamper and an inking pad. Very carefully he adjusted the wheels for the month and day, then conscientiously pressed the stamper on his pad and with the greatest care impressed it upon my passport.

"*Ausreise. Bundesrepublik Deutschland. Zollzweigstelle Eschebrügge – Kanal 1*," I read, followed by the date. The day and month were correct, but I noticed that the figure for the year was five years out-of-date.

"Excuse me," he said as he began to reset the numbers. "You see, the traffic on the canal is not very heavy."

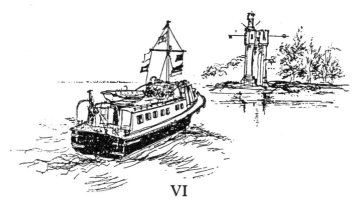

VI
Windward of the Law

T he police inspector looked at me stiffly.
"The Wasserschutzpolizei does not accept bribes," he declared.

During her twelve years on the continental waterways *Commodore* was never in real trouble with the police. When interviewed at Georgsdorf on the Left-Handed Canals she was treated with precisely the kindness and consideration that was right and proper, and she in turn was pleasant and forthcoming. Her difficulties with the police were usually of quite a different kind – how to get them off the boat.

The men of the German Wasserschutzpolizei were in the early days of her travels usually men who had served in the wartime German Marine. They loved boats and they liked to relax and chat. But there was one other thing they were passionately fond of, and that was tea. This originated in many of them having been in British prison camps after the German collapse in 1945, and a British prisoner-of-war camp (as Hans Kruse had also discovered) was no bad place to be in during those months of semi-starvation. At the end one went home fit as a fiddle, and also addicted to the habit of tea breaks with a good strong cup of tea that was better than litres of anaemic beer. I first discovered this at Bremerhaven where we had the WSP on board for a couple of hours before one of them stood up and said he really must be going. And he went – to fetch his wife to join the tea party.

The non-taking-bribes affair happened on the Rhine. In 1960 I had run *Commodore* as close as possible to Oberammergau so that we could travel down to the Passion Play, which I had already attended on three earlier occasions. That meant pushing her up the Main into Bavaria to the limit of navigation, which in those days was at a shoal just below the Schweinfurt railway bridge. But with such a long voyage so far from her Dutch base it also meant finding some place where she could safely be left for the winter. Down below Frankfurt I began to call at anything that looked like a boatyard, but there was always some curious reason why they could not take her in. Reaching the Rhine I tried all the harbours near Mainz, and though none could help me I was recommended to a certain Herr Bauer or Meyer, or some such common name. I found his wharf further down river, and even if I did not take an instant liking to the man I arranged for *Commodore* to be left with him and slipped before the cold set in, and covered over with tarpaulins. Relieved to have everything properly arranged I next got to work to do all those necessary things to guard against frost, emptying the hot and cold water lines, draining the cylinder and stove, and dismantling all the cooling pipes and pumps about the engine. I had just finished these tedious jobs when there was a slight bump as a police boat came alongside. Two officers stepped aboard, accepted a cup of tea but seemed at the same time to be worried about something.

"Come over to our boat," one of them said to me mysteriously. "We can talk there without being seen or heard."

As I followed them into the blue cigar haze of their saloon I wondered why they were so furtive. I sat down at their table and offered them each a fresh cigar. Then I waited.

"You are leaving your boat here?"

"Yes."

"How long for?"

"The winter," I said.

"We thought so. Of course it is no business of ours, but have you signed an agreement with Herr Meyer (or Bauer)?"

"No. Not yet."

"You have not signed anything, is that so?"

"Why yes," I admitted. "I can do that in the morning."

The men exchanged glances. "You must understand that the Wasserschutzpolizei would never blacken a man's character. Never. They are quite impartial, and unless a man is a convicted criminal they would never express a view which was in any way deprecative of any person whatsoever."

"Quite so." I could not get the drift of this conversation at all.

"That being the case we can only say as members of the WSP that Herr Bauer (or Meyer) is an admirable man, hard-working and without any known flaws in his character."

"Ah! I'm glad to hear it," I said.

"Wait." One of the men held up a hand. "It is our duty to say so. The WSP is impartial and would never blacken any man's name...."

"Exactly."

"But if we were not members of the WSP we would tell you that Herr Bauer is the biggest scoundrel unhanged. However, such opinions must not pass our lips."

"Besides," added his colleague, "If we were not men of the WSP sworn to look upon other men as worthy citizens until proved otherwise we might add that when you returned in the spring everything of value would have disappeared off your boat and Herr Bauer would swear that those things were never on board. However, we must say nothing other than that Herr Bauer is no doubt an excellent and reliable man."

I understood. "So you think I should move?"

"Why not? You have signed nothing."

I told them how hard it was to find a place at all, but they said they knew a spot some way further down the Rhine. It was an excellent place – they could safely say so, even as men of the WSP force. Honest, reliable, the proprietor did maintenance work on the police boats. But of course as WSP men they could not take it upon themselves to recommend him.

To move at once was not so simple, because I had to reassemble all the cooling pipes and strainers. I explained this, and said I would certainly do it but maybe it would take me an hour. They then pointed out that an ordinary man who was not an officer in the WSP might regard Bauer as a man easily moved to anger, if not to violence. As soon as he was no longer in view they would back away, I would slack off our lines, and they would then take the inner berth with us outside them. There we would be safe, as the worthy Bauer could only reach us across their boat, which he would not dare to do.

The unsuspecting boatyard proprietor was soon seen driving out of the yard on some errand or other, and the police boat took the inside berth. I then started putting back the pipes and priming the pumps, and when all was ready I knocked on the side of the police hull. In a moment they flicked off their lines and ran out speedily stern first, with *Commodore* still lashed alongside. Out in the river they took the children aboard for a speedboat ride and put their powerful craft through its paces while I followed them down the Rhine to our destination, which proved as satisfactory as they had hinted.

Now it struck me as remarkably kind of the water police to take the trouble to save *Commodore* from a man whom between knocking-off time and early next morning they allowed themselves to regard as a very unsavoury character, and when I went in to town the next day I took with me one or two jars of coffee and a box of tea-bags. We were going home by train that afternoon and there was no point in leaving these goods on board to become stale. At that time good coffee was not to be obtained at all in Germany, or only at a ridiculous price, and tea was at a premium too. So I thought it would be a pleasant way of thanking the WSP if I took this gift to their headquarters for the use of all the officers there.

The WSP base was enormously impressive, and its upper windows commanded a view of a busy stretch of the river. Several empty speedy craft lay at the police moorings, rocking on the heavy wash of the ceaseless traffic plugging up the stream, deep laden from Rotterdam or Duisburg, and the roof of the building bristled with radio aerials of all shapes and sizes. The floor of the entrance hall was polished like a mirror, and as I mounted the stairs to the control room I wondered if my shoes were clean enough.

The Duty Commander in smart black uniform turned to look at me, his eyebrows asking my business. I explained that I was enormously grateful for the help and advice given me by two officers, and as I was about to catch the evening train to Hoek van Holland I hoped that he, on behalf of the WSP would accept some coffee and tea with my thanks.

It was then he looked at me so stiffly.

"The Wasserschutzpolizei does not accept bribes!"

"But it isn't a bribe," I stammered. "It is just to say thankyou. You might call it a gift."

He regarded me sternly. "Gift or bribe, it is the same. The Wasserschutzpolizei could never accept any such thing."

"What a pity," I said. "This coffee and tea will not be much good to us when we return next spring."

"Probably not," he said, as though he was not particularly interested.

"So the only thing I can do with it is presumably to throw it in the river."

"Wait!" He rose from his chair, and I wondered if he were going to produce a file of regulations about the penalties for polluting the river with houshold refuse. But no, he smiled to me pleasantly. "You misunderstand me," he said. "I merely said the Wasserschutzpolizei cannot accept a gift. But it can happen from time to time that something may be discovered upon the premises for which there is no reasonable explanation. Something may be found, and yet none comes forward to claim it. These things do happen." He turned and called in a commanding voice toward the next room.

"Meyer!"

A middle-aged office policeman hurried in. "Yes, Sir?"

"Meyer, is your personal locker in the basement locked?"

"Yes, Sir. I always see that I leave it locked correctly."

"Then go down and unlock it."

"Certainly, Herr Kommandant!"

The man hurried out of the room, and the Commander started to ask me in the most casual way about our trip during the past year. We talked for a minute or two, then he called another assistant in to the room.

"Take the Herr to the basement," he said.

"Yes, Sir."

"Wait outside until he has seen whatever he wishes, then bring him back upstairs."

So I was led down to the basement. My companion opened a door and I found myself in a room the walls of which were lined with steel lockers such as one might see in a railway station. They bore numbers, and all of them were closed except one in the third row, which stood wide open to reveal a rain-coat and one or two personal odds and ends. Officer Meyer was there too, standing in the corner like a punished schoolboy and looking at a blank piece of wall.

My guide closed the door behind me. Meyer did not move, but I understood what was expected of me. I placed the jars of coffee and the packet of tea-bags on the shelf of the open locker, and as I went to the door to leave the room Meyer sprang to life, slamming the front of his locker, turning the key and putting it in his pocket. Then the two men led me back upstairs.

The Commander shook me by the hand most warmly. So did the other officers. They wished me a pleasant journey home and a happy return in the following spring. Honour and a strict code of behaviour were satisfied.

★ ★ ★

Once when coming down the Moselle I drew in as usual to the wharf at Bernkastel-Kues, one of the very few landing stages of any use along all the German section of the river. It was a pleasant position, about twenty minutes walk from the town and twenty seconds from one or two little Weinstuben where small vintners served their own production. We had not been at the quay above an hour when a woman came to the hatch, carrying a receipt book and with a leather money bag round her waist. She had come to collect eight marks, she said, for our mooring fee.

I had never paid at Bernkastel before, nor so far as I can recall had I paid at any public quayside in Germany, France, Holland or Sweden. I had always believed that one gave sufficient recompense to the local authority by patronising the butcher and baker and grocery-shop, and I believe so still. I have never taken kindly to the idea that private boats are milk-cows to be pumped out by the town-hall staff, and on this occasion I said I was not going to pay. The wharf had, to my knowledge, been there for many years and it did not belong to the good woman any more than to me. As for the town, what extra facilities did it provide in return? None whatsoever. No, thankyou, there would be no marks forthcoming.

The woman was naturally surprised, but not even the statement that the few other boats had paid up like lambs did anything to mollify me. "You mean to say, if I stay alongside the quay I have to pay?"

"Yes. Eight marks. It is the regulation." She was adamant.

So very naturally I cast off, and anchored the ship some ten feet away from the wall. The collector was non-plussed by this action and was not quite sure what to do about it. The situation was solved for her by the arrival of the WSP in their smart boat, returning from a day's surveillance of the river. Seeing *Thames Commodore* lying off they wondered what was the cause.

"Engine trouble, Sir?"

"No, not at all. But I would rather not lie along the quay."

"I see, Sir. Why do you prefer to be in the stream? It is not easy for you to go ashore. You would need to use your dinghy."

I agreed. "But you see, they expect me to pay eight marks if I lie alongside," I explained.

"Eight marks? Ridiculous!"

"She says it is the regulation charge. And what are they charging for, anyway? Nothing at all. It is unblushing robbery."

"Quite right, Sir. All the same, in your present position you might be somewhat in the way if a big transporter from the Ruhr came in for the night. Perhaps it would be better if you were to move – but not to the quayside of course. May we offer you the use of our own staging instead?"

Such a reasonable, helpful attitude was typical of the water police, and I appreciated it. Only once did I meet the letter-of-the-law attitude which one might expect German police to have, and that was when we had been up the Colmar cut in France to show Ingrid the imcomparable Grünewald masterpieces in the Unterlinden museum. On our return to the Rhine we chugged ahead for a while and then cut across the river to a place where there was a pleasant little harbour run by a local boat club. We had hardly settled down before a police launch drew alongside.

The composition of the crew was curious. There were four officers on board, for the Rhine being also the boundary between French Alsace and German Baden it was considered sensible to have two French police (in dark blue uniforms) and two Baden police (in green ones). This dual authority made it easier to cope with land contacts on their respective shores and it was also a demonstration of the entente between the two lands – though very typically the French officers had been selected from an area where German was not spoken and they understood not a word of that language any more than they did of English. It can only have been national pride that lay behind such an absurd arrangement, I think, but it certainly drew out the proceedings because everything that the Germans asked, and my replies to them, had to be translated backwards and forwards. An even more ludicrous arrangement was that the two police forces had their own established times of coming on duty, taking breaks and the like, but they worked on different clocks. The French operated Summer Time but the Germans did not, so when it was midday in France it was only eleven o'clock in Germany, but time for the police boat to take the Frenchmen over the river and leave them ashore for the lunch break. So far as I remember, the Germans broke off for lunch from one to three, and it was nearly tea-time in France before the French officers could be picked up again.

When they had all come aboard, the senior German officer took command. He was a keen young man, about twenty-five with a somewhat forceful manner.

"You have been navigating the Rhine. Have you a pilot?"

"No," I said. "I never take a pilot."

"Then I must see the papers."

I produced the registry document, which was beautifully written in teachery script. There were plenty of figures on it, but he could make out the gross registered tonnage of twenty-nine.

"Over fifteen tons you must have a pilot."

"My dear man," I said in perhaps a rather patronising tone. "I have been navigating the Rhine for seventeen years. You had hardly left the Kindergarten when I was already on the Rhine. Nobody has ever told me before to take a pilot. I am perfectly capable of managing the Rhine by myself."

All this now had to be translated to the Frenchmen, who looked embarrassed and sat back to light cigarettes.

"You may not proceed on the Rhine until your boat has been inspected and certified as suitable."

"Then you may inspect it," I said.

"No, it is not for us to carry out an inspection. The inspectors are in Mannheim. There will be a fee of three hundred and fifty marks to pay, and you will also pay the return travel first class from Mannheim. There will be two inspectors. An appointment here will be arranged within a few days, perhaps next week. Meanwhile you will stay here."

It was important not to lose my temper, but I felt the Pilk blood pressure rising. "There is no need to trouble the inspectors," I said. "This boat has been over the Channel and the North Sea, across the Baltic, down to Spain, and for that matter up and down the Rhine more than once. It is obviously a sound ship. Anyone can see that immediately. I can assure you that any inspection is unnecessary."

"You will have the ship inspected," he answered firmly. "Then a certificate will perhaps be issued and you may go on your way."

"I can go on my way without your permission," I said as gently as I could. "The Rhine here is technically the Grand Canal d'Alsace. Even if a pilot and inspection were necessary lower down, that would not apply here. The river here counts as a French Inland Waterway and is outside the regulations for the Rhine as a whole."

I knew my facts about the Rhine. Under the Treaty of Versailles France had been empowered to take or divert the whole river down to Lauterbourg where it became totally German, and to dam it and use it for hydro-electric power. They had to provide locks and to pass all shipping free of charge. The locked sections, even if in the original river bed, were described as the Grand Canal d'Alsace.

"I also have a Certificat de Capacité," I added. It was the one that had been issued to me in exchange for a bottle of whisky. I went to my cabin to fetch it. The German police looked at it, but said it was no good for the Rhine, only for French Inland Waterways.

That was precisely my point. Even if we were sitting in Germany the Rhine here was by definition a French canal, and so our route to the Mediterranean lay clear ahead, and they could not stop us.

But the officer wanted to go on with his questioning. "You have navigated the lower reaches? Where did you come in to the Rhine?"

"At Koblenz this time, but I have run it all several times, from above Basle to Rotterdam. And never been stopped until now," I added.

"If you have had an uninspected ship and no pilot that is a serious matter. It will be a matter of investigation and prosecution."

"I think you would do better to investigate thoroughly why all the German police between here and the Dutch frontier never raised these matters before," I said. "I have met police-boats all up and down the Rhine, and never had anything more than a courteous wave or salute." This remark nettled the young man, whose colleague sat throughout the proceedings without doing more than nod confirmation whenever it was required.

"Show me your passport. And that of your wife."

We produced them. He put them in his brief-case. "I shall take these," he said. "I shall consult my superior and return after lunch." The superior was presumably a land-police inspector somewhere nearby.

It was an ingenious way of preventing our crossing over to France. Trying to look pleasant I said he might take the passports and ship's registration, and that no doubt his French colleagues had seen him do so.

It was now time for the Frenchman to be taken over to the Alsatian shore for lunch. It would be some hours before the Germans returned from their consultations, followed by their own lunch break. Ingrid decided that it would be wisest to have our own meal and await the outcome of their deliberations rather than annoy them further.

The German police had not long been gone when a man jumped down to a neighbouring pontoon from his motor-yacht which was moored there. He had evidently smelled trouble and came round to see what was in the wind. We shook hands, and he introduced himself as Herr Waldvogel.

"That's an unusual name," I said. "I knew a Herr Waldvogel fifteen years ago. He was a wood-carver in the Black Forest, and he carved a wooden dish for our daughter's wedding."

"My brother," he said. "I remember his carving the names too. So, welcome to our port! And what are the police making trouble about?"

I told him. Reduced to its essentials the problem was first that of tonnage and fitness of the ship to be on the Rhine. Apparently *Thames Commodore*

On duty bound. The Wasserschutzpolizei always at your service.

Top: The official re-opening of the Strömsholms Canal.

Bottom: Commodore in Hallstahammar Locks on the Strömsholms Canal.

should have been certified, or tuberculin tested or something, but I was not going to pay for a couple of civil servants to joy-ride down from Mannheim to do it. And there was also the matter of pilotage. For any ship of fifteen tons or over, pilotage was compulsory on the Rhine, it seemed.

"Did you not know that?"

"Well, yes and no." I had heard of the regulation, I told him, but I had never bothered about it because when first I started running the Rhine the rule did not exist. It was evidently assumed that if you could reach Germany from overseas in your own boat you would be perfectly capable of knowing which side of a buoy to steer. And if it was originally in order for me to be without a pilot, then surely it must be in order now.

Waldvogel smiled. "You do not know the German official mind. But we will find a way out. I know that young chap. He's not so bad really. We play skat together every week in the pub." He seemed to be thinking. "Come and sit in my saloon. When they come back I will invite them in."

In mid-afternoon the two Baden officers took their cutter and went across the stream to pick up the Frenchmen. Then they all four came back and walked along the jetty towards *Thames Commodore*.

Waldvogel went to his hatch. "Come in, come in," he called. "the company are here."

The four officers came in and sat round the table. The two French policemen were trying to look as though they were not responsible for what was happening, as indeed they were not. They looked around them, intent on admiring Waldvogel's boat.

"Beer?" Waldvogel had a case handy and he held up a bottle to the Frenchmen, who nodded appreciatively. He poured out a couple of glasses while the Germans glared at their colleagues for being so indiscreet.

Our host poured out for himself and us, then turned to the Baden officers. "Beer?"

"No." Evidently they did not accept bribes, but Waldvogel took no notice. He poured it out just the same and pushed the glasses over to them.

There began a brief and awkward period of platitudes, and Waldvogel dropped in some remarks about how wonderful it was to have somebody coming by boat from England, all the way to their little harbour. I had been to the Main, too. Even to the Weser. Had the officers been to the Main? No? Never mind, they could read about it instead. The Herr Kapitän of the *Thames Commodore* was enthusiastic about it. He had written in praise of it. The book was in German too.

The French were rather out of their depth, so Ingrid went to fetch one of the "Small Boat" books which contained a charming David Knight sketch of Strasbourg. They were enchanted.

"Strasbourg! Oh, what a beautiful city," they said. The Germans ought to go and see it one day. Ingrid then turned over pages to another David Knight, which showed two officers whizzing through the shipping in a boat of the Wasserschutzpolizei.

The French were almost hysterical in their amusement, and they showed it to the Germans, whose pride at having their service illustrated was noticeable. We could also see that the officer who had made the complaint did not know quite how to tackle the matter in hand. He had arrived stiff and full of threatenings and slaughter but now he was desperately trying to think of a way out of the unpleasant position into which he had got himself. He was sure that he had a case – as he had. But at the same time he did not want to be the one to start arresting a harmless individual who had obviously written enthusiastically about his country. Nor did he wish mortally to offend his fellow skat-player of Friday nights. He looked out of the window, hoping against hope that he was going to be summoned on some other matter, but none was looking for him. Several times he looked as though he were going to speak, but he could not begin.

"Drink up, man," said Waldvogel. The two Germans took a minute sip, a tiny bribe, that is to say.

"The English are mad," Waldvogel declared. "Feet and inches, miles, pounds, ounces, nobody can make head or tail of their measures. They insist on being difficult, and having their own units. It's obviously the same with tonnage. If they say ten tons they don't mean ten tons at all."

The officer looked at him in surprise. I saw the drift of Waldvogel's idea and I nodded. "Quite right," I said. "It's as bad as the Swedes. I wanted once to buy some cans of beer, and when I asked how far it was to the village a man told me it was two miles. I walked and walked for a couple of hours and never even saw a sign of the place. That was how I learned that a Swedish mile is ten kilometres, whereas when we talk about a mile we mean one point six kilometres."

"There you are," said our host expansively. "Just as I told you. By the way, what tonnage does the ship's registry certificate state for our friend's boat?"

The officer took our paper from his brief-case. "It says netto, twenty-three point four-six."

"Ridiculous!" Waldvogel laughed and filled up the glasses for the French, who could not quite follow what was going on and so had decided to look at some more of the David Knights. "Twenty-three! What did I tell you? I imagine their English tons are about half ours, what?"

"Yes, of course," said the officer, seizing the opportunity so ingeniously offered. "Yes, yes. That must be so."

"Of course it must be. But now tell me, what do *you* think *Thames Commodore's* proper tonnage would be?"

The policeman looked out of the window toward where she lay. Then he smiled. "Thirteen," he said cheerfully. "Certainly not more."

We all laughed, and the tension relaxed. I explained the joke to the French officers who were politely intrigued. They cared more for David Knight's pictures of places on the Meuse than for mathematical semantics.

Waldvogel opened some more beers. We received our passports and ship's papers back, and sat for a while talking of boats, and the Rhine, and how good the Alsatian wine was – this to cheer up the Frenchmen, who were a little left out of the fun. Eventually the German police decided that it was time to go off on patrol again.

"Just one moment," I said as they were climbing aboard their boat. "*You* understand that when it says twenty-three tons on our paper it really means thirteen. But others might not realise that. Supposing we go down the Rhine again and are asked our tonnage ...."

"It's thirteen," said the officer. "That is agreed."

"Yes, but if we are asked for the ship's papers? There the figure is twenty-three."

He grinned. "Then I should lose the papers."

He signed to one of the French, who started up the motor. Evidently it was their turn to be in command, and a moment later the international crew was shooting out of the port to surge away down the Rhine. Or, to be correct, down the Grand Canal d'Alsace. And shortly afterwards *Thames Commodore* headed upstream to turn out of the Rhine below Basle, cross the Belfort Gap and drop continually down until once more we could drop anchor, put down a ladder and jump overboard into the clear, warm, sultry Mediterranean Sea.

★ ★ ★

For years the boat had no real base, and any craft needs some sort of place where she can rest in the winter. She had wintered recently in Holland, in Sweden and even at Teddington where she was built, but we needed somewhere for her to lie so that with increasing age we could speedily reach her from Jersey and have a leisurely voyage of a week or two without a long haul before we reached what we wanted – hills, flowers, walks on mountain paths with French bread and paté and a good bottle of local wine, and a strong smell of history. Eventually we found an ideal place on the river bank at Aigues Mortes in the Camargue.

It is impossible to say that one waterway or one little village is more attractive than all others. People have often asked me which is my favourite canal, and this is a question without any possible answer except that I have no overall favourite at all. The candidates for top place are far too many. All I can say is that none appeal to me more than .... And then would follow a long list of perhaps a dozen or more starting with the

Strömsholms in the north and ending with the Midi (or 'Canal Royal des Deux Mers en Languedoc', to give it its proper title) in the south.

The same is not quite true of the places upon them. For example, repeated destruction by fire on the one hand and over-enthusiastic socialist planners on the other has had the result that in Sweden there is hardly a country town which is anything more than a sterilised piece of uniform boredom – and I say this as one who loves Sweden dearly, so very dearly that the sight of what enlightened planning has done to it can make me weep. One of the glories of France is that such matters as sewerage and road fly-overs are not allowed to ruin a place. It is not so much a matter of conscious preservation as of not permitting matters such as hygiene to destroy the quality of life or the age-old cat-alleyway charm of a village.

I first saw Aigues Mortes in 1962, on the old *Commodore's* last voyage. Its charms were then less known than they are now and there was no park for tourist buses by the canal basin. Nor were there any hire fleets based there, or within hundreds of miles. It lay slightly decayed, a sort of minor Carcassonne somewhat lost in the mosquito-infested marshes of the Camargue. Times have changed and Aigues Mortes now has a continual flow of summer visitors, yet it has not lost its character. It is four-square within a mighty continuous wall so high that not even the television aerials stick up above the ramparts. The sides are pierced with narrow gateways, and no authority has been foolish enough to widen them or smash them down. Outside the gate nearest the canal basin two benches are placed again the bastions, and there the older men sit throughout the day in the sunlight tempered by the filtering of the plane trees, and talk of the same matters that occupied them yesterday and the day before.

Through this gate the main street leads straight to the central square a mere hundred yards ahead. The bakery on the left has the best baguettes, the one on the right our favourite croissants, but there is no cheese worth eating. For that one must wait until Sunday when the market vans are ranged along the northern wall to fold down their sides and display a delicious range of paté, spices, olives, butter, melons, and endless kinds of cheese from all the varied regions of France.

Down the street there are of course shops with black cowboy hats and sea-shells and tins of marzipan sardines, but how should there not be? On the left is the ancient, unornamented church which has undergone little change in the last six centuries and is one of those where the hundreds of years of devotion fill the simple nave with an atmosphere that is tangible, almost overwhelming. For in the thirteenth century Aigues Mortes was built as a fortified commissariat base and departure point for the crusades led by the gallant, flaxen-haired young Louis the Ninth – a man so exceedingly pious (according to his biographer) that if anyone blasphemed or took the name of God lightly he had their tongue bored through with a red-hot iron. His noble bronze stands in the square, close to the same church where his armoured nobles from all of Western Europe knelt one by one for the blessing from the Pope's envoy before they embarked to sail down the cut (at that time much shorter, for the sea has since receded) to the Middle East. Some were rapacious, some no doubt wanted to impress the girls they left behind them, but many were moved by a burning zeal, however cruel or foolish to our modern way of thinking the expression of their faith may have been.

The square has groups of tables and chairs belonging to various cafés and small restaurants, and these are kept under constant watch in the morning by sparrows and later in the day by scrounging dogs which have a definite protocol as to which may snatch half a slice of bread dropped off one of the tables, or a bone surreptitiously thrown underneath by a diner. Meanwhile children splash each other with the water which dribbles into stone basins from the spouting dolphins at the feet of St Louis or play out the soft southern evening with hopping games whilst their elders eat.

At the beginning of October there is a new activity in the square. Enormous cauldrons are heated up, filled with gallons and gallons of fish soup which will be served to the pensioners at trestle tables ranged in front of the town hall. It is a sign that summer is over and something else is on the way, the festival of Aigues Mortes. Already the tourists and swallows have left and the busiest place from dawn to dusk is now the wine co-operative outside the walls. Tractors driven by the sunny-natured men of the wine-fields drive to the weighbridge and back their trailers to the pit where an Archimedean screw relentlessly pulls the bunches of grapes into the crushing rollers. There is a delicious squishing sound, and a strong scent which is not quite that of wine, for as yet it has not developed its alcohol. Across the road and against the south ramparts the local people are assembling a collection of three-or-four-tiered structures which look like family pews with several storeys. This is very much what they are, for they will be fixed to their neighbours to form a ring of private spectator boxes, except at one point where a small public stand is included. In the arena every day throughout the festival the local lads can enjoy their favourite sport of being chased by relatively harmless bulls, just as their ancestors did when the Greek settlers introduced their bull games nearly two thousand years ago. This is not bull-fighting, but a contest in which animal and man match their speed and dexterity, and if the bull would perhaps not mind butting a man on his bottom no onlooker would ever sanction cruelty from man to animal. And so natural and long established is this relaxation at the start of winter that no effort is made to attract visitors and not a centime is charged to anyone who may like to sit in the public stand, socially less exalted than in a family box and more draughty if the mistral is having a day of exercise.

The bank of the cut opposite the south-west corner of the walls and across from the vintner's co-operative was to become *Thames Commodore's* permanent home for the winter. It was an excellent place too, for it provided the opportunity to cast off and head eastward to the islands off Toulon or up the Rhône, south-west to Spain and the foothills of the Pyrenees, and westward to that beautiful waterway the Canal du Midi, a canal of which the allure becomes even stronger for me year by year.

In 1981 this famous sea-to-sea cross-country waterway celebrated its tercentenary, for it was on a day in May of 1681 that the Royal Commissioners, the Cardinal Archbishop of Narbonne and a collection of other bigwigs accompanied by a band of musicians set out eastward by water from Toulouse, followed by twenty-three laden barges. Nothing could have been more wonderful than to repeat the splendour and pageantry with another procession of boats three hundred years later. But it was not to be. With remarkable lack of imagination the central waterways authority had decreed a *chômage* on the canal and over that particular date most of the canal was drained of water for its annual period of maintenance. A chance that would not recur for half a century had been missed.

Nevertheless a celebration was planned at the summit level, where the long feeder-stream cut three centuries earlier from the Montagne Noire debouched into the canal. There at Naurouze the 'Friends of Pierre-Paul Riquet' (he constructed the canal) had arranged for a new plaque of bronze to be unveiled by Mlle Eveline Riquet de Caraman, who I believe was the last survivor of the line of the great canal man himself. The plaque was a fine one, presented by the Inland Waterways Association and beautifully cast by one of their members in the English Midlands, and I had personally taken the heavy object down to the Midi by car when putting *Thames Commodore* in commission a month or two before the unveiling.

A busload of IWA enthusiasts came down from England for the ceremony, and one or two members of the American Canal Society were with them. Of course it was ridiculous that the whole affair could not have involved a flotilla of boats but it often happens in France that one hand of the government does not know what the other hand is doing – and perhaps does not greatly care. It was a pity for ourselves also, as I had intended that *Thames Commodore* should personally honour Pierre-Paul Riquet, Baron de Bonrepos, by being in the right place at the right time, but as that was going to be impossible the best we could do was to avoid much of the closed section by running out to sea, turning toward Spain, and entering the branch canal at La Nouvelle forty miles down the coast. There was water in this branch as far as Narbonne, and as that was to be the overnighting point of the IWA party we could lie between the oleanders in the centre of the town, prudently upstream of the discharge pipe from the public lavatory, and keep open house on board for the canal enthusiasts in the evening.

The occasion at Naurouze was as different as could be from a Swedish canal centenary. Quite apart from having to accept a half empty canal-bed there was no state governor, no proclamation from the president. A number of people sufficiently local to know where the mill of Naurouze might be found came to stand around under the lime trees, and the mayors of two nearby villages were there too. But there was no Cardinal Archbishop of Narbonne, whose predecessor had worked so strenuously in support of Riquet at the time of the canal's construction, no brass band, no dancing on the village green. For that matter there was no village green. All the same it was a happy occasion, and after the unveiling the children from the primary school of a nearby village sang to Mlle Riquet de Caraman a song in honour of her illustrious ancestor.

Two days later the sluices were opened to fill the canal from end to end. It was the Sunday afternoon when we set off from Narbonne to reach by nightfall the point where on the following morning the water would have arrived and navigation was to be resumed. The La Nouvelle branch was both narrower and shallower than the main line of canal and along this section it was advisable to keep well to the centre to avoid the projecting roots of the bankside plane trees. It happened just then to be the close season for coarse fishing in the Department of Aude, but one fisherman was there just the same. He had a little grey Renault beside which lay the quantity of miscellaneous gear which a canal angler seems to require. As we approached he began to shout and gesticulate and sign that we were not wanted.

I am, I think, careful to be courteous to anglers and to try always to see where their lines are, and to slow down so as not to stir up too much mud. But no slowing pleased this particular individual. He reeled in his line, and as we came slowly up to where he sat he seemed busy with his gear. What he was so occupied with was to put a heavy weight and hooks on his line, and just as we were abreast he served it at us with all his force. The lead struck me so hard just below the shoulder that it knocked me off the steering stool on to the deck. If it had hit me on the head it would without doubt have been fatal, but luckily it did not. And by astonishing good fortune the hooks missed both of us.

Scrambling up, I stopped the boat, but at this the man began to collect half bricks and cobbles from the canal-side track and we deemed it unwise to come within range. And when I took up my camera and tried to man-oeuvre to get a front or rear view of his car he threw up the one end in the air, then stripped his jacket and placed it over the other number-plate. Ingrid took a somewhat distant photo of him, but as he bent down to show nothing but a large trousered bottom this was not much use.

There was not a house nearby from which to call the police, so we chugged ahead. We thought my arm was broken, but by the time we reached the next lock twenty minutes further up the cut we were sure it was not. However, the arm was something of a mess, so before dressing it Ingrid took some colour close-ups of the injury in case they could be used as evidence. At the lock the lengthman, who was off duty, got out his little 2 CV Citroen and took me bumping away down the tow-path to catch the man, but by then he had half an hour in which to make himself scarce, so we were not surprised that neither the man nor his car were any longer there.

This was not the first time I had been a target, but the other occasions were many years earlier and in England. Once it was a boy on Lambeth Bridge who took up a bag of gravel temptingly placed at the parapet by the road department, and dropped it. Luckily I saw it coming and pushed one of our passengers clear. The second time was a milk bottle flung by a youth in Reading. One can expect such things occasionally from idle youths, but the carefully calculated attack by an angler was something new to me. And something so out of character for one who can sit placidly on the towpath for hours on end that both Ingrid and myself wrote the man off in our minds as a psychopath and left it at that.

Yet news has a curious way of travelling along canals, and next afternoon we were summoned to the telephone at a lock thirty kilometres further on. The divisional engineer wanted to speak to me. He did not like people to be assaulted on his waterway, he said, and he asked me to lay information to the police, and to give a detailed description of the fisherman. He said the lengthman had a suspicion as to who it might have been. The engineer also advised me to send a copy of the report of the grave and criminal assault to the British Embassy in Paris, who would push to see that action was taken. This was soon to show how little he knew of the British Embassy in Paris, which proved to be most accomplished at polite hand-washing and referred me to the consulate in Marseilles, which told me not to expect any action but enclosed with their best wishes a list of English-speaking advocates in Marseilles.

So I wrote to the police at Narbonne and enclosed the juicy coloured photographs of my arm and another showing a distant Renault with the tail door in the air. I expected some sort of acknowledgement, but none was received. I had forgotten the incident when in February of the following year, nine months after our encounter with the angler, a letter arrived from the Tribunal of First Instance in Narbonne, requesting me to be there the following week for a 'confrontation'. Narbonne was a long way from home in Jersey, so I asked that the affair could be held over until July, when I would be on board somewhere in the neighbourhood. Then, one summer's day I betook myself to the court, where I was ushered into an office to have a private preliminary hearing with a very pleasant, sandy-haired young man in shirt sleeves who was the examining magistrate.

There was a secretary present to type out statements, and in case I had difficulty in explaining myself a very competent, suntanned and extremely glamorous interpreter.

On the way by train from Carcassonne I had gone over in my mind all the questions I might possibly be asked. At least, I thought so, but there I was wrong. After the formalities of name, age and birthplace the magistrate asked me how long I was incapacitated by the attack.

"I was not incapacitated at all, Sir," I answered.

"But you must have been."

"I was not, I can assure you."

He was very patient with me. "This is a case of grave and criminal assault. Grave and criminal assault inevitably results in the victim being incapacitated. You must have been unable to work."

"I am retired, really," I said. "I am 'Third Age'."

"Yes." He checked my age in the file. "But when you are not retired, what are you doing? What is your occupation?"

"I am a writer, Sir."

"There! So you could not write, because your arm was injured."

I shook my head. "I write with my right hand. The injury was to my left arm."

They all laughed. We were getting nowhere very rapidly.

The magistrate considered. "Well now, let us say you could not write as you usually could. It was difficult. Perhaps you were unable to apply yourself properly to your profession. In other words *you were incapacitated!*"

He was so insistent that I had been made either a physical or mental wreck that I let him have the point, and it was duly entered on the report.

The magistrate turned through the papers in the file, then laid them down. "For how long were you incapacitated?"

"Oh, not long."

"How long? A few days? Or weeks?"

"Not weeks. A few days, perhaps."

"Ah." He nodded. "About a week?"

"Yes, if you like." I was anxious to oblige.

"Good. You say about a week, about eight days. Was it more than eight days, or less than eight days?"

"Honestly, I was not so injured that I was counting the days......"

He smiled again. "Quite so, naturally. But were you incapacitated for less than eight days or more than eight days?" He was insisting on an answer.

"What does it matter?" I asked ingenuously.

"Because it is like this," the magistrate said in his kindly shown-to-the-children voice. "If it was less than eight days, then it is a matter for this court. If it was more than eight days the case has to go to a higher court."

"I see. Well, now you ask, I recall that it was about four days," I answered.

So with that point of the court's competence established we could proceed with the case. There was to be an identity parade. Could I still identify the assailant if I saw him? I could, I was sure.

"Now, Monsieur Pilkington, I have to explain that the police have brought in the man they suspect. He was brought in last February when we wrote to you, and has been warned to appear when you are in Narbonne. The police are reasonably sure they have the assailant; but at the same time other people have expressed the view that he would never do such a thing. And of course he says so himself. But if you are ready, we will proceed with the confrontation."

Three men came in and stood in a row. The one on the right was a man of about forty with a moustache. He had police-sergeant written all over his features. Next to him was a man of well over seventy, bald except for a fringe of whitish hair as though he were a monk. He would not have hurt a fly. I could rule him out too. On the left was a heavily built man of perhaps thirty-five with a sallow complexion and jet black hair parted in the middle and coming down thickly at the back of his neck. I had no doubt at all which was the man.

"Well? Are you ready to make a choice?"

"Yes. The one on the left," I answered.

"That one?" The man was told to raise his hand. "The one with his hand raised?"

"Yes."

We all signed a lot of papers about my choice and the three men filed out.

"Well, Monsieur Pilkington." The magistrate smiled pleasantly, but looked puzzled too. "The man you chose is a police officer."

I smiled too. "Perhaps. But do you know how he spends his Sunday afternoons? He might be a very keen angler."

The magistrate liked that. But then he explained that the man brought in by the police was the elderly fellow in the middle. They considered that it was he who had attacked me.

"It couldn't be," I said. "He's short, over seventy, red-faced and bald. My description says about forty years of age, heavily built, about one metre eighty, pale face, thick black hair parted in the middle – exactly like the man I selected. How could they bring in that poor old fellow?"

He sighed. "Yes, he is certainly nothing like the description you provided. I will tell the police to try again."

I thanked him, and the interpreter and the secretary, and I asked him not to bother any more. I was more sorry for the old chap who liked fishing by the canal and must have lived for months in the fear that he would be wrongly identified as my assailant. If nothing else, my visit to Narbonne must have been a relief to him.

VII
Troubled Waters

A river has a fascination for the boatman. He can see it as a mysterious spirit, beckoning him to explore ever further, with the result that he can be so carried away with its beauty and its romance that he wants to see round just one more corner.

That was how the Thames affected me. Downstream from Maidenhead it was an easy run to Windsor with its castle and the wide stretch of the Long Walk up the Great Park, and all the glory of Eton across the stream. Or going up river there was the crisp beauty of Winter Hill on a frosty morning, the peaceful slow bend of the Thames above Hambleden Mill, the grandeur of the reach by Mapledurham. But always I wanted to go further, to pass another lock or explore the canal links to either side, to head down through the docks of London to the widening funnel of the estuary under the grey, leaden skies which so often seemed to stretch over it.

And yet the same waters that can enchant a boatman with their beauty, their history and romance can have a more sombre effect upon another individual. Looking down from the bridges that span any great river one can see the water as a silvery path to adventure, but one may also find there a rolling stream of oblivion, a mysterious entity offering peace, forgottenness, an end to those thoughts which destroy the hours of sleeping as of waking.

During *Commodore's* voyages on the Thames in the late nineteen-forties I often met the boats of the Thames Division of the Metropolitan Police. Sometimes one of them would draw alongside when I was lying against a lighter, waiting for the tide to turn or a dock to open, and it was on one of those occasions that I learned about the unfortunate men or women who jumped off the bridges into the turgid river below. At that time suicide was still technically a crime and only mentioned furtively if at all. Chad Varah had not yet founded the Samaritans, and the general understanding of depression was in its infancy. Nevertheless the Thames Division coped with attempted suicides from London's bridges in a way which was not too legalistic and was, I think, humane and sensible.

Jumping off bridges was practically confined to Westminster and Waterloo Bridges, and hardly a night passed without a case of it. The favourite time was after midnight and especially around two o'clock in the morning, and the police were so used to the behaviour of an intending jumper that it was rare indeed for anyone to be drowned. It is hardly likely that anyone so depressed as to want to put an end to his life will take the bus or tube to Central London, walk straight to the river, stride to the centre of the bridge and promptly vault over the parapet. There is indecision, a walking to and fro from end to end of the bridge, stopping to peer over the balustrade, hesitating. All this may be genuine indecision of a person who is really wondering whether to put an end to it all, or it may be the act of a 'cry-for-help' individual who wants to appear to try to take his own life but requires a long time before jumping so that he can be certain he has been seen by the police and will not be left to drown.

And the police have indeed been notified. An officer is somewhere near either end of each of the two bridges and he has spotted the individual with the macintosh drawn tight over his neck, walking up and down, peering, stopping, starting again. The officer has already sent his message, "Jumper on Waterloo" or "Jumper on Westminster." The message does not go to a police car but to the pier of the Thames Division at Charing Cross. A boat is kept ready, the engine warm, the ropes ready to flick off, and within seconds of receiving the warning it is moving out to hover in the stream. The officers see the figure at the parapet, they watch him climb at last to the rail and then drop into the river. He has hardly hit the water before the searchlight beam has picked him up.

It is curious that even a determined suicide usually shouts for help as soon as he is in the water, and this appears to be some sort of direct reflex reaction to the cold – and perhaps the taste – of the water. The help is already on its way, the jumper is hauled inboard and taken down to Charing Cross Pier, which is specially fitted out with a bath, a good supply of hot water and a clothes drier. By the time a male jumper has properly warmed up again his clothes will be dry, and then it is time for a cup of tea. (Spirits are not provided. If it became known that to get a free double Scotch after closing time one only had to leap into the Thames, there might be a queue of jumpers.)

While the tea is being drunk a relative is sought out to come and take the jumper home. However, there is (or at least there was when I learned about it) one difference in the case of female jumpers. Modesty prevented the men of the police boats from stripping a woman of her wet clothes. She was dumped in the hot bath fully dressed and handed over warm but dripping to whoever had been summoned to take her home. But in either case that was the end of the story, and no trouble was made for the individuals concerned. They had had enough already, and probably the depression which caused the night-time leap into the water would be there the next day, as dismally strong as ever.

It was on the Seine just upstream of Conflans Ste Honorine that I realised that what I took to be a log awash had a belt round it. The body was floating in a frog-like position, face downward. I turned, secured the woman with a rope, and as I did so she rolled over and I saw her face. She was neither beautiful nor ugly, but had an expression of astonishing calm, a peace as though all her troubles were over and she could forget all the unpleasantnesses which had haunted her. The face was serene, and there came into my mind the jacket of a book I had read thirty years before, *Die Unbekannte*, the unknown woman. There too the face of the drowned woman had looked out from the rippling surface of the water in the same absolute serenity.

The body was that of a thick set woman of over forty, and she was wearing a skirt of blue-grey tweed and a jersey of dark blue with a black belt. She had a gold wrist-watch and a necklace chain with a small medallion. And although her face struck me as so composed, at peace with the world, this was probably due to the relaxation of the muscles and the disappearance of wrinkles in the swelling.

Some weeks later I was told by the Conflans police that she was a certain Henriette Gillet of Courbevoie, further upstream. She was aged forty-nine and had suffered from depression to such an extent that she had tried on several occasions to drown herself, but her relatives had always prevented her.

"You know how it is," the inspector said, putting his thumb to the side of his head and working it to and fro like a corkscrew. "She was not mad, but..... You understand?"

I did, and I did not. I had no great experience of depression, or of the rejection it evokes in others. And it is this rejection which may drive a sensitive person to the end of their tether. People get tired of the gloom, the moaning and groaning, or the introspective silence. The depressed person is forced in upon himself, the problems loom larger, the depression becomes clinical or critical. The end may not be far away.

It was only a fortnight or so before I saw another body bobbing up and down on our wash as we went up the Aisne toward Soissons. This was a less pleasant sight because the man's head had at some time been struck by a barge propeller. Again I turned, roped the body and towed it up to the next lock. And what struck me on this occasion was that all along the river people were watching from their suburban windows, yet when I called to them to phone the police they either shut their windows or in one case said they had no telephone, although I could see the wires on

the side of the house. Even after it was all over, a suicide was rejected.
Alive or dead, people wanted to wash their hands of the indecency of
suicide. When Ingrid and I found a young man in a backwater of the
Rhône at La Roche Glun we drew over to beside an angler, pointed to
the body and asked him to go and telephone, but his only response was
to pull in his line, place a fresh maggot on the hook, cast again and stare
at his float. This body was expected, the lock-keeper told me. The man
was aged thirty-two and had jumped in at Tournon a week or two before.
It was a case of depression.

Although some depressions are inborn and permanent, or caused by
biochemical factors (the Soissons man was affected by the drugs used to
counter a fever which he caught when serving in Indo-China) most of
them come from the weight of problems falling upon shoulders that are
not strong enough to bear them. Marriage troubles, financial loss, bereave-
ment, sexual deviations, loss of a homosexual lover, sheer loneliness because of a retiring nature, these are only a few of the causes which can
bring about depression. To treat it with some sort of oblivion-inducing
drug can cover it over and perhaps hold it back, but the really lethal
influence is the absence of anyone to talk to, anyone who can accept the
person without just telling them to pull themselves together and snap out
of it. Obviously that kind of admonition is just foolish, for nobody who
could possibly pull themselves together unaided would fail to do so. But
it is more than foolish. It is quite likely to be the last straw of rejection,
the final word that drives a confused and helpless individual to walk to
the middle of the bridge, hover in hesitation and then jump over. The
brilliant insight that came with the founding of the Samaritans was that
the depressed and suicidal person simply needed befriending.

★ ★ ★

Water itself may have a certain fascination for the sad and despairing,
so it is not surprising that in the many years of voyaging I came upon
several of these unhappy people. But there was another somewhat menacing
aspect of life upon the water, and that was the latent, hidden possibility
of being unintentionally caught up in what are euphemistically known as
'cases of industrial action'. It was not that the barge community resented
my using their canals; very much the reverse, a fact which often surprised
me.

"You are amusing yourself, but we, we are working." This was stated
to me by a French barge captain after I had asked if I might draw in
alongside him. It was not said with rancour or jealousy but merely as a
statement of fact which was indisputable. I was amusing myself, but
navigating the canals was for him a matter of his livelihood. Even before

he had put the difference so simply I had always tried to tell myself that however frustrating it might be to wait behind a plodding barge it was not reasonable to race past it and cut it out at a lock which was ready and waiting, nor to be impatient when the man ahead eased right off so that his wife could exchange all the gossip of the year with the woman of the barge coming in the opposite direction. They were working, I was amusing myself with (in their estimation) all the time in the world, and to have an attitude which accorded with this difference was always appreciated. Or nearly always.

Of course there might occasionally be a boatman who regarded yachts as the toys of capitalist layabouts, but as many a bargemaster was himself an entrepreneur with a ship that might represent a value of a hundred thousand pounds, they were more concerned to work on the maintenance of their capital asset whilst waiting for a cargo than to fritter away the day in jealousy. The barges that became more and more run down until they had to be abandoned probably reflected the fecklessness of the skipper and perhaps difficulties within the family, and they seemed to involve couples who had failed to make a succes of anything on dry land and so, either in a moment of faint optimism, or for lack of other opportunity, had acquired an ailing craft and had become overwhelmed by the difficulties of leaks, cold, breakdowns, and time lost. And there could be the drink problem on a barge as anywhere else.

As bargemen were in many cases privateers – and mobile ones at that – it was not likely that any considerable solidarity of a trades union type could easily be established to present a united front in matters of rates of transport, working hours and the like, so the bargeman was at a disadvantage compared with a lorry-driver or railwayman. Besides, he had no regular place of work, no address where he could be asked to vote in any kind of ballot. His barge might carry the name of a Dutch town on the stern but the skipper would be signing a contract at the counter of a freight bureau in Burgundy to carry a cargo of grain to Mannheim in Germany. Yet in spite of these difficulties a sort of general frustration could sometimes begin to grow, spreading mysteriously over part of the network of European canals until something happened.

When I had agreed to run *Thames Commodore* from the Mediterranean to the Meuse so that the Flemish Television could make the film of an English ship on a Belgian river I was faced with a very considerable voyage. Up early and running till the locks were closed for the night it could not be done in less than three weeks, I thought, and three weeks hard labour with very little time to enjoy all the charm and beauty of the countryside and the towns and villages on the route. There would be no stopping to see the Palace of the Popes at Avignon, the excellent Roman museum at Lyon, no chance of walking in the Alpilles, in fact nothing but plodding along like a barge that was working. It would be much better to continue amusing myself, by taking twice as long over the trip and dividing it into three holidays with a selection of friends and relations. Having decided to do so I arrived by train at Agde, where *Thames Commodore* had spent the winter, had her hauled out, scraped and painted below on the slipway used by drifters, and next day I set off alone for the voyage of two or three hours out to the sea and along the coast to Sète. I never had any difficulty in running her single-handed, except that it was hard to make tea below decks unless one could put the helm over and turn circles, which I had done on various open stretches of water when no other craft were dangerously near.

At Sète I made fast and rowed up through the mighty lifting bridges to the railway station to pick up my cousin Elisabeth, who was another with a slight touch of water on the brain. She had had a boat on the Aylesbury branch of the Grand Union, and when I met her in Switzerland she happened to mention that the one thing she had always wanted to do was to go up the Rhône. Or down it. This was a stroke of luck for myself and I at once signed her on to make the trip with me a few weeks later. In 1973 the most difficult sections had not yet been tamed or regulated and to run the whole river alone would have been daunting, so I was delighted to have the company of somebody who could steer, and had a great amount of sense in boating matters.

To aim for the north we had to go inland at Le Grau du Roi, turn through Aigues Mortes, strike the Little Rhône near St Gilles, reach the main river just above Arles and then head up for a run of a few more hours to Avignon. That was enough for the first two days and in the afternoon we walked up to what has always been a favourite outlook of mine. Past the fortified ferocity of the papal palace, up by a broad zig-zag allée and between the rose-beds to the great summit of the Rocher des Doms we came to the edge of the great rocky lump which towered above the Rhône where it twisted and swirled at what used to be its swiftest point along all its course, round the end of the famous Pont d'Avignon of the song, standing broken in the river. Further away beyond the Villeneuve branch of the stream (nowadays the navigation route, with a lock) the mighty fortress of the Fort St André shone white in the sun, the huge bastions awaiting an invading army or probably a team of cinema technicians intending to use it yet once more as the setting for some great romance of war and love in the Middle Ages. All this we admired as we stood under the clear Provencal sky, and then, looking down at the river, I saw a boat, white with a blue line below the deck, a boat with beautiful lines having a short bowsprit and a mighty mast lying back over the whole of its length. I knew her at once, and it would add even more to the pleasure of our voyage if we were to have the company upstream of Irving and Exy Johnson in *Yankee*.

I had first met that remarkable sailor Irving Johnson several years earlier below Duisburg. He was going up the Rhine, I was steering down, so I turned and stemmed the current while we conversed through loud hailers and the great Rhine ships went thrashing by on either side. Since then I had met him – usually going the opposite way – in a number of improbable canals and had even prevailed upon the Johnsons to come round by our little harbour of St Aubin in Jersey. Years later Ingrid and I were to stay with them in their home on the Connecticut River and see, among the museum of extraordinary things brought from all over the world, the ship's wheel at which he had stood and steered round the world not just once, but seven times.

Yankee had been designed and built for the Johnsons. She was a remarkable ship, for she could pass the French canals and bridges – even the Canal du Midi, where *Thames Commodore* had no more than an inch clearance on two of the bridges – and yet could sail any sea and travel round the world. By using the gang-plank as a fulcrum Irving could wind up his heavy mast with no assistance except from the anchor winch, and everything about the vessel was planned with a view to ease of working without the interference of paid hands. As she now headed for the quayside above the Pont we hurried down to meet her. Next day we set off together up the great river.

It was unusual that we met no traffic coming downstream. Nor for that matter was there any commercial shipping going up as we were. This did not immediately strike me as strange, because very often there was little traffic on the Rhône, and one could happen to be in a period when very little was on the move. But at one of the great locks the engineer said that we would not get far up the river. There was trouble, he said, and the route ahead was blocked. Irving was as determined as I was to press on, for we could hardly imagine a landslide or any other phenomenon which could block the Rhône so entirely that we could not squeeze past it somehow.

At the next lock we had no response to our arrival other than a continued red light. Nothing seemed to be coming down, so I went ashore to climb the tower and ask if we might go through. The keeper was sitting with his feet up, reading a book. He did not like to be disturbed. Obviously there was domestic trouble at home, for he was uncivil and refused to open up his lock for us, but he gave no reason. Maybe he would open later, he said, and that was the most I could extract from him.

I returned aboard and we waited. A cargo ship coming upstream would have forced him to press the buttons, but there were none, nor any coming down. An hour passed and a return visit to the lock office brought out nothing but a display of angry temper. Back on board I recalled that as a young man Irving had toughened up his nerves for sailing round Cape

Horn before the mast by standing on his head on the top of a telegraph pole. I had seen a photograph of him actually doing so.

"Why don't you entertain him by standing on your head on the bowsprit, Irving?" I said. "He might like that."

To my amazement Irving walked forward, and although he was then in his mid-sixties he put down his head on the sprit, kicked up his legs and waved them in the air. I hooted toward the lock and the keeper looked down. But the effect was not what I had hoped. He left the cabin, locked the tower, got into his car, slammed the door and drove off.

Another hour or two passed until the next keeper came on duty, a pleasant young man who at once took us in and raised us to the top level. I asked him about the lack of traffic and he said it was a strike. Not of lock-keepers but of barges. He thought we could perhaps make Lyon but there was no information. Beyond that he was sure we could not proceed. The barges had blocked the river, and according to his morning paper the whole French network was immobilised by blocking the waterways at twenty-two strategic points.

We made Lyon with neither difficulty nor traffic. We came up to the Saône, which was to be our route to the north, and there ahead of us a double line of barges was moored. Tied abreast they stretched all the way from bank to bank of the wide river and one could hardly have squeezed past the end of the line in a kayak.

The strike was for higher freightage rates. It had only been on for a day or two, but tempers were already frayed. One reason, I discovered, was that the only water tap in the neighbourhood was on the wall of property belonging to one of the freight agencies and the management had decided to turn it off at the main. Understandable but unwise, I thought. An action of that kind could only annoy – and the position of the women on the barges was already more and more inconvenient the further they were situated from the end of the line of the town side. To buy a baguette those furthest across had to hurdle up and down over the sides of thirty ships before they reached the quayside and could walk a quarter of a mile to the shops. To give them a similar extra distance to carry buckets of water was not likely to mollify them.

I went back to Irving and asked him to take down his ensign, the Stars and Stripes. I knew that the Johnsons were sensible people, but the same might not be true of all the barge community. This was a period when France was suffering from occasional and irrational outbreaks of anti-American feeling (one can never forgive people for generosity, it seems) and I did not want any stones thrown at *Yankee*. After that I decided to see what could be done to have us allowed to pass the blockage.

There was a strike committee of eight skippers, and they were meeting in a pub. A barge captain told me how to find it, so I left Elisabeth on board and went there. The men were sitting around drinking beer and smoking cigarettes. It just looked like any other gathering of barge men, and not at all like a revolutionary council of war. I introduced myself as captain of the blue yacht and asked if I could join them. Somebody offered me a beer. Later I paid a round too, but I did not want to appear patronising by doing so immediately.

At this time there was a celebrated trial going on in Lyon. For technically impeccable reasons a local woman doctor had defied the law and bravely said she was going to carry out an abortion, which she did. She was promptly arrested and charged with murder or manslaughter or something of the kind. From the conversation among the men I gathered that one of them, a friendly and rather rotund man with a marked squint, was pressed for space on his boat because he had eleven children, even if some were away at a residential bargee school, probably at Conflans-Ste-Honorine. I thought it would be interesting to hear his views on abortion, which was a matter which sometimes came my way because of its far-reaching effects both before and after, and because I had also been on a commission of the churches looking at that and similar problems in the neither white nor black but rather murky grey areas of human sexual behaviour.

The subject proved to be a winner. The strike committee was happy to discuss the morality of such an affair and they became more and more relaxed. Most but not all of them supported the lady doctor in her action, and when we had pumped out the subject sufficiently and another round of beer was on the table I raised the subject of yachts. We had nothing to do with fixing freight tariffs, I said, we all loved France, and every day more and more yachtsmen would be prevented from taking their holidays in the south if somewhere or other they were stopped. It would make no difference one way or the other to the negotiations with the freight agencies if the shippers let private boats through. The barge men might certainly refuse to load or carry, and that was well within their rights, but there was no reason to interfere with others outside the quarrel. Of course I knew that this view of mine was not exactly trades union logic, but how twisted that logic could be astonished me when the chief man of the committee explained it.

The branch official of the Transport Union had taken command of things locally he said. Most of the skippers did not belong to the union for the practical reasons I have already mentioned, but somebody had to co-ordinate things across the country and the Transport Union had taken on the task. The local official in Lyon had said it was vital to stop yachts. There could be no exceptions. And seeing I was puzzled the bargemaster went on to explain that Monsieur Quelquechose of the Union had said that stopping yachts was their strongest card. Everyone knew that Monsieur Edward Heath was a great yachtsman. He would be sorry to hear that other yachts were suffering frustration, so sorry that he would at once contact Monsieur Pompidou and beg him, or tell him, to instruct the freight agencies to give in to all the demands of the skippers.

The idea of Monsieur Heath and Monsieur Pompidou weeping on each other's shoulders over the trials of yachtsmen stuck in French canals was too ridiculous, and yet typical of the lunatic notions which union men can sometimes develop in themselves and actually believe.

I laughed.

The skipper was surprised. "You do not believe it is true?"

"I'm sure it's true that Monsieur Quelquechose thinks that Mr Heath has nothing better to do than to worry about my boat, but I think the monsieur should see a psychiatrist. I have heard a lot of idiotic ideas in my day, but this one takes the biscuit."

Some of the men thought I was right, but they were powerless. The union had taken control, and Monsieur Quelquechose was coming to the quay at two o'clock to address the crews of the barges in the blockade. Maybe I would like to come. After all I was a skipper like them, was I not?

Shortly before the time of the meeting the barge people at the outer edge of the blockading line began their journey up and down over the rails and across the hawsers and hold covers of the craft between them and shore. We all hung about on a loading area by the river where a mound of gravel provided a suitable rostrum for the union man who was to address us. When he arrived he turned out to be a pleasant man of about thirty-five who looked much too elegant to have risen from the workshop floor or lorry-driver's seat. He was smartly dressed and had a natty briefcase. Clearly he was an office-socialist, and I noticed that he was received with a certain degree of tolerant apathy. He climbed to the top of his pyramid and began to address the meeting.

It was hardly fire-raising stuff, his speech, and there is no need for me to try and recall the platitudes about solidarity and exploitation. He ended by striking one fist repeatedly into his other palm as he made his final declaration that the all-wise union was right there behind them.

"Friends! Let me assure you on behalf of the union – which has your interests very much at heart – that none of you will be losers by the blockade. I am very well aware that many of you are losing precious time by being immobilised in the common interest. You are losing your daily bread, going without the hard-won means to support yourselves and your families." I thought of my friend with the eleven children.

"Yet I declare," he went on. "I declare that there will be no loss or damage to any ship stopped by our industrial action from voyaging on its lawful business. None, I repeat, none shall suffer any loss. If there is damage, then the union will compensate you. Let us stand together, and in firmness achieve victory!"

There was a little mild applause. The speaker was pleased. He raised his hand for quiet.

"Are there any questions?"

A hand went up. It was mine.

"Yes?"

"Does what you said about damage and compensation apply to yachts?"

He was unprepared for that one. He looked around for help, and somebody said to him that it was the captain of the blue ship down the bank there who had asked the question.

"I do not understand the question," he said.

"I asked if it applied to yachts when you said that none would suffer loss or their ship be in danger. Does it apply to yachts, or does it not?"

I glanced at my neighbours of the strike committee, who were clearly amused. The speaker looked toward them for guidance. They nodded their heads affirmatively.

"Yes, it does," he conceded.

"Thankyou," I said.

"No more questions, anywhere?"

My hand went up again. He wondered what was coming next.

"There are several yachts held up. Two more have arrived since I reached the blockage this morning. There will be more every day, coming up the Rhône. Many of these people are on their annual holiday. They will have to leave their boats in Lyon and go home. You say none of them will suffer loss or damage. How can the union ensure that? Do I understand that the skippers of the commercial craft will undertake to look after the yachts until the end of the strike?"

Again the official looked hopefully at the strike committee, but again they nodded approval.

"Yes," he said. "The captains will look to the care of the yachts."

"Thankyou," I said. "I will call at your office after lunch and ask for it to be confirmed in writing, so there is no doubt."

When I had done so, Elisabeth and I consulted with the Johnsons. We could not continue our voyages, and we did not believe the assurances that within two days the freight agencies would have given in – pushed, no doubt, by Monsieur Pompidou to oblige Monsieur Heath who was suffering from lack of sleep because we were stuck in Lyon. Irving and Exy were on their way to pick up a charter party, so the blockade was a serious matter for them. However, for some freak reason the strike did not extend to the Canal du Midi and Irving immediately secured a large hire cruiser and ran his trip on that waterway instead, leaving *Yankee* in Lyon. Elisabeth and I abandoned ship and flew home.

It was more than six weeks before the bargemen threw in their hand. They had gained nothing, and lost six weeks of pay. I doubt if the union compensated them, but when I returned to Lyon *Thames Commodore* was safe and sound. The men had been as good as their word, and no yacht had come to any harm at all.

★ ★ ★

Three years after the great French barge strike we were on our way home from Karlstad in central Sweden, which was the nearest port to Ingrid's family home in Värmland. The voyage took us by way of the Trave, through to the Weser and thence by the Ruhr. For the final stage of our journey we were joined in Germany by our ex-god-daughter Rosamund Horwood-Smart. She was in chambers as a barrister, and highly competent on board too, for she had been a sort of acting chief officer on voyages of two or three weeks for several years in succession.

Our voyage went splendidly. Down the Rhine, through Zeeland, turn right at Hansweert, follow the estuary down to Terneuzen and there turn in to the Ghent Ship Canal. The entrance lock at Terneuzen was of a size to accommodate the ocean-goers which frequented Ghent and I was surprised that we had it all to ourselves, for the traffic was usually very heavy on this link between Belgium, Northern France and the Rhine, yet even on the ship canal itself not a vessel was to be seen.

As usual I drew in at the Belgian frontier, and took out a ticket to go through Bruges and onward to Dunkirk. "I think you are wasting your francs," said the clerk. "There is a strike. The canal is blocked at Ghent."

Soon we came to the blockage. There was a mass of barges of all shapes and sizes along the quays on either side, and a ship named *Sorry* moored sideways across a gap in the middle as a movable boom. Just beyond them was a railway bridge. A harbour launch came through the small gap in the blockade and hailed us in perfect English.

"You want to go through, Sir? We'll take you through at eleven o'clock when they have swung the rail bridge. There will be three ships coming the other way first. When they have passed we'll take you through."

Later in the morning a small detachment of the Gendarmerie climbed over the barges to the one moored in the middle. They cast off the ropes, paid no attention to the flaming young female revolutionary left in charge of the ship, and then started up the motor and drove the barge out of the way. None of the boatmen attempted to interfere in any way, not even by shouting.

The rail bridge was slowly swinging. Three Dutch Rhine-ships came round the bend and ran through the gap. On each of them there was a man in uniform with an automatic rifle standing on either side, fore and aft, and a fifth beside the steersman. I could see that the authorities were not going to stand any nonsense, but I did not want to get mixed up too closely in a dispute which involved having ships protected with machine-guns.

The harbour launch swung round, signed to us to follow, and led us up toward the city. Once clear of the blockade they wished us a pleasant voyage and took their leave. The whole route ahead was clear, they said.

But there they were unaccountably wrong. The next day brought us round the edge of Bruges, past the windmills in the park to the Damme-poortsluis, the only lock between us and Ostend. I had almost forgotten about the strike until we came upon a mass of barges above the lock. The way to the gates was not actually obstructed, but as we drew up ahead of the lock there was shouting and running and one or two men jumped off their barges, hurried over the lock-gates and came to where we lay against the bank.

Their leader was a stocky, determined fellow. Next to him stood a stout, red-faced man in overalls. Then came a bald-headed thin man with gimlet eyes and rimless spectacles. The other two were youngish and rather droopy men of the kind who agree with everything that others say. Their leader began to address us in a mixture of French, Flemish and German. The gist of it was that we were not to go any further. No ship had done so for five weeks, he said. One or two had foolishly tried and perhaps their owners were now sadder and wiser men.

The others nodded approval. Yes, it would be dangerous to try. It would be much better to do what another yacht-owner had done. He had been stopped too, but the skipper had the sense to go home – here they pointed to a sailing-yacht registered at Hull, which lay by the bank, locked and empty. We should do the same. Our boat would be all right where she was.

"You really advise us to go home?"

"Yes, yes. You go home."

"All right," I agreed. "Go up to the town and buy three return air tickets from Brussels to London for tomorrow. Oh, and three rail tickets from here to Brussels, while you are about it. And pay for them, don't forget."

The strikers were obviously surprised. As I was turning to go below as though to start packing up, they explained that they were not going to buy the tickets. I told them that in that case I was quite happy to go on, but not just now. We were going to start cooking supper. And I bade them goodnight with a smile. We now had the whole evening to plan our next move.

As soon as I appeared on deck next morning the delegation came over, and they asked if I was leaving for home? Not just yet, I told them. Bruges was an interesting place, there was plenty to see, and maybe we would stay a few days as – who could say? – the strike might soon be over. Only I would need to tank up with fresh water to see us over our staying. I said this for a good reason. I had been through Bruges often enough and knew where the tap was. It was situated half way along the lockside.

When I walked up to the lock office the troupe followed me in. There were four lock-keepers, as there were plenty of paddles to be worked and a road swingbridge also, so a sizeable staff was needed. The men were playing cards, as they had been doing for weeks past, and they were surprised that anyone should wish to go through. But they were willing enough to open their lock for me to water up and I asked that they would also lower me to the other level. The canal was not so congested there, and I thought the mooring would be better. Somewhere near the brewery lawn, I suggested.

The head lock-master asked if I intended to go on down the canal, and I answered that eventually I would do so. I would turn just short of Ostend and take the Canal de Plassendale to Furnes, on the way to Dunkirk. I said that I had read about Furnes, and what an interesting little town it was with its procession of hooded penitents and so forth. (That was perfectly true. The book in which I had read about Furnes was actually written by myself.) Was it not a good idea to go that way?

One of the lock men knew Furnes and said I would like it. In fact I had been there four times already, but that was not the point. Every word I said was carefully noted by my audience of strikers, and I could well imagine that they must be delighted that I could be so foolish as to say I would go that way, for the canal was not so broad that men driving down the service road could not hit us with bricks and other missiles. Besides, it passed a number of old-fashioned swing-bridges attended by aged women, and even if the ladies could not be terrorised into refusing to open for us the actual navigation gaps were so limited that assailants would be within four or five feet of us on either side. Of course I was well aware of this too, but the red-faced striker thought it wise to point out what might happen to us, and in so doing he unwittingly gave away the delicate position they were in.

The strike had already been on for five weeks. It was in fact a Belgian strike, but some of the ships were French *particuliers*, owned by their skippers. They had been willing at first to join the strike to help their Belgian brethren but by now they were becoming restive and wanted to leave. I gathered that the Belgians had managed to block them in; but, as this man so ingenuously revealed if any boat should escape the French would be up and away too. That was why we must not be allowed to pass.

There was one fact which set the strikers minds at rest and convinced them that we could not escape. About three hundred yards below the lock there was a swing-bridge, a massive one on a main road. If the bells began to clang and the barriers to drop across the approaches the men would

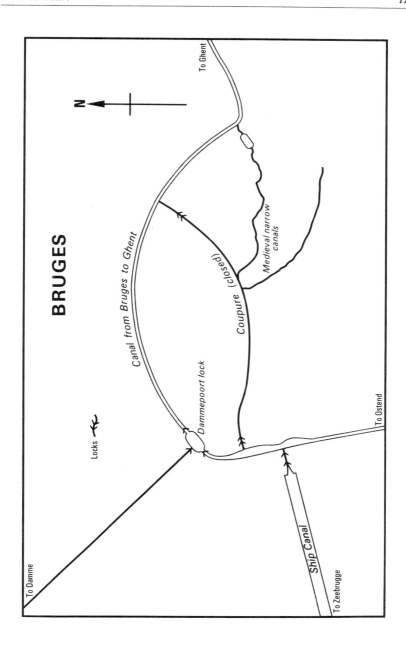

BRUGES

N

To Ghent

Canal from Bruges to Ghent

Medieval narrow canals

Coupure (closed)

Dammepoort lock

Locks

To Ostend

To Damme

Ship Canal

To Zeebrugge

have ample warning that we were off down the canal, and they could chase us by car. Many barges had cars aboard, and some of these had been run ashore during the strike and were alongside their boats.

So the lock was opened for us, we filled up with water just as I said we should, and with the lower gates opening the strikers ran off round the lock to catch up with us again. While they were away for a minute or so a tall and very solid man in a trilby hat came to the lockside ladder. He was just as I had always pictured to myself Simenon's Inspector Maigret, and when he quickly showed me in the palm of his hand his identity pass as a detective officer I was not very surprised. The lock staff had phoned and he had come to tell me that it would probably be unwise to force an issue at the moment. Tempers were running very high, which was hardly surprising among people who had been stationary for five weeks, sitting in their own sewage. The French were impatient to be on their way. The strike was cracking. Give it a day or two to see what would happen, then perhaps everything would be quiet, he advised. But the discovery that the unfortunate French skippers were being detained against their will encouraged me to try to escape.

The spokesman of the strikers had now reached us by making a tour of the lock. He told me I was not to go to Furnes that day. I said that did not matter at all. I would go some other day, maybe. Never mind, there were so many things to see in Bruges. The Memling museum for instance. I had never had a chance to see that, and I was in no hurry to go to Furnes. What I needed just now was to find a good berth where we could lie up.

The man was obviously relieved, and he said I could probably find a good position on the bend below the lock near the brewery lawn. So I thanked him, and the four lock men, and moved slowly out of the pen, whispering to Ingrid to tell Rosamund not to look nervous but to smile and wave whenever possible, and to keep their eyes and attention concentrated only on the port bank. They both looked wonderfully relaxed as we came up to the brewery lawn. I went forward, sounded with a pole and shook my head. We moved on some yards. No, not here. I held my nose and the ladies shook their heads. It genuinely smelled atrocious, not only from chemical effluent but from the weeks of combined slops and sewage of a hundred or two barges. We crept on, all our attention on the shore and quayside to the left. We were up to the return bend now, and I could see out of the corner of my eye the bridge on the starboard side. I knew that it crossed the entrance lock of the Zeebrugge Ship Canal. The gates were closed but unobstructed. I told the ladies not to glance toward it, just keep indicating any possible space on the other side of the canal. Gliding at dead slow we passed the entrance.

"Hold on tight" I called. And at the same moment I went full speed astern into the lock entrance and brought up by the gates. We were safe. The bargemen could not block us from the lock if they tried.

There was some shouting, and the committee came running to the lock and were quickly joined by a union official, an elderly man in a macintosh who bore an astonishing resemblance to Nikita Kruschov. He began to entertain us with cautionary tales of how barges had been smashed up and ruined for trying to make their own way. Tar, paint, refuse and petrol had been poured on them from bridges. Windows had been smashed with bricks and cobbles, paving-stones had crashed through wheelhouses, smashing the accommodation. Several craft had even been sunk. He was an excellent story-teller and I tried to look suitably frightened. Then Rosamund did the act which we had arranged in whispers.

Rosamund liked acting, and she could look a very purring and slinky pussy-cat if she put her mind to it. She staggered up to the deck with a large sack of rubbish, and all smiles she willowed up to Kruschov and asked him where the rubbish bin was. He was flattered – I think he liked her perfume, too – and he trotted away with her to find a rubbish bin. She thanked him for being so sweet, and left him at the bin. Watching for the moment when he turned the other way she darted in to the lock-house and asked the elderly officer to open the gates. He dared not do such a thing, he said. The men might attack the lock. He could not take such a responsibility.

Rosamund wheedled him and he phoned the port captain at Zeebrugge. This official told him bluntly that if a ship wanted to pass the lock it was his business to help it to do so.

The Zeebrugge Ship Canal was not a part of the Belgian national waterways system. It belonged – as I well knew – to the port of Bruges-Zeebrugge. It was not filled with blockading barges, and in fact I could see nothing in the waterway beyond the lock but one or two cargo vessels discharging at the quays. And because the canal was outside the network it was outside the strike – just as we in fact were. The quarrel was between the barges and the government, over conditions, rates of carriage, the cost of fuel and so forth. Besides, the ship canal was under 'marine regime', and accepted orders from the authority of the port of which it was a part. So, somewhat reluctantly, the keeper told Rosamund he would open the gates for us.

While this was going on a tall, thin Dutch skipper in light blue overalls had arrived by the lock-gates and he and Ingrid were having a very useful conversation. He had at first joined the strike in sympathy, he said, but now he was fed up with it. To try to stop us was ridiculous, he agreed. Apart from being unfair on ourselves it certainly would not help the strike. An incident involving a foreign yacht would stiffen the government's resolunion to have no truck with the strikers. But he wanted to tell us that after five weeks of useless strike and lost pay the bargemen were in a dangerous mood. His private advice was that we should not move the boat without protection. Maybe if I could contact the nearest British consul he could arrange to lay on a covering force of Gendarmerie.

Taking the shopping bag and enquiring rather loudly how much milk we needed and whether we needed bread for lunch, I set off into the town, intending to rustle up a British consul somewhere in Belgium by telephone. On my way I happened to pass the Gendarmerie, and I went in.

"Ah," said the inspector. "Monsieur the captain of the *Thames Commodore*, yes? The port captain at Zeebrugge telephoned to say you were intending to use the lock and he requested protection for you. A mobile detachment has already been despatched to the lock."

I hurried back, turned the boat and ran her through the gates, which were open and waiting. On the one side stood Inspector Maigret, on the other two handsome young men with automatic rifles, staring up into the air as though watching the swallows chasing the midges. Beyond them were the five men, the spokesman and the bald one, the ruddy and rotund skipper and the two droopy yes-men. No cobbles flew, but the Dutch captain winked to us from the bridge parapet.

We dropped down, and the bottom gates opened. Beside them stood Kruschov in his macintosh. Rosamund waved to him pleasantly, but there was no response. Inspector Maigret jumped into his little blue Renault and drove along the service road. The ship canal was far too broad for us to be within range of a missile from the bank, but three miles down there was a swing-bridge and he halted there to stand beside the engineer. He was taking no chances.

At Zeebrugge also we saw him visit the office of the harbour lock. Then with a reassuring wave of his hand and lifting his hat to the ladies he turned and drove away. *Thames Commodore* passed through the gates of the tide lock and chugged out into the freedom of the seas.

As for the strike, it persisted for a few weeks more, although I suspect a few of the Frenchmen managed to escape too. In a desperate attempt to wring concessions from the government a party of wives travelled up to Brussels to put their case to the Queen. But Fabiola wisely refused to interfere. The strike collapsed.

A year later I was talking to a Belgian skipper on the Meuse about the strike. It had cost him one fifth of a year's takings, he said.

"But did you not get what you wanted?"

"No." he laughed. "The only concession was that we should not be allowed to work on Sundays. Previously we ran until the locks closed at lunch time."

"That was not much of a gain," I said. "It merely means that as an owner-captain you lose half a day's running and half a day's profit every week. If my mathematics are correct that means a reduction of approximately seven per cent in your earnings."

"Exactly," he said. "That's just what I calculated myself."

Waulsort Quay

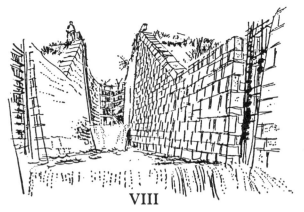

VIII
Reopened with a Bang

F rom Germany to Scandinavia there were two links. Both led into German Baltic waters, from where Denmark was a mere afternoon's trip distant. Each route proved to be a lesson in itself. The Kiel Canal with its ocean-goers thrashing its water night and day was a demonstration of mammoth engineering, but the river Trave from Lübeck to the sea proved to be a lesson in humanity. On the one bank the individual was there to serve the state, on the other the state was run for the benefit of the individual.

If anyone should think that there is no difference between these outlooks I would recommend to them a trip down the Trave, provided they keep course between the left bank and the middle. On the western side romantic couples walk arm in arm on the beach, grandpa snoozes in a deck chair while the grandchildren race in and out of the shallows followed by a delighted family dog. A group of young people is picnicking or singing to a guitar in the sunshine. A conscientious daddy is showing his toddler how to design a really successful sand castle. Across the river and within a mere two hundred yards there is a a dead shore without so much as the sound of a bird. There is plenty of barbed wire, however, and every here and there a watch-tower rises above the trees. One can make out the occupants. They have powerful binoculars, and guns, and are ready to shoot at anything or anyone foolish enough to try to escape from the benefits of a life under the successors of Marx and Lenin. It is a terrifying contrast, and after I had steered down the Trave I found it impossible to forget the spirit of hatred and fear which brooded continually over the right bank of that boundary stream. I was relieved to reach the open sea and breathe again the fresh, half salty air of the blue Baltic Sea and set course straight up for Sweden.

To reach Sweden one has to thread a course through the multitude of Danish islands, low, sandy and flat. They are not dramatic but are pleasant enough with their small harbours, the village streets of houses painted in green and ochre, brown and red. Great brick castles stand on bases of glacial boulders, and immense steadings as well as a tang of manure testify to the prosperity of those who breed cattle and pigs. It is an old world country, but because of its consisting more or less of sandbanks slowly raised from a receding water level Denmark is not in any way a country of inland waterways. There are large sounds and pretty inlets where the fields and trees dip their toes in the half salt water of a tideless Baltic Sea, but apart from the harbour cut at Odense the only other canal I ever discovered was the one leading to Naestved in southern Sjaelland, which is one hour's navigation in length but has no locks. And in Copenhagen there is a lock with no canal – its purpose being to prevent a current through the city when the water level changes with the wind. So, Denmark making so poor a showing as regards waterways, we can run in and out of its isles and keep our sights on Sweden, two days ahead. For curiously enough Sweden is one of the finest canal countries in Europe.

Our first Swedish harbour was Helsingborg, straight across the narrows from Hamlet's Elsinore (Helsingör) in Denmark. The buildings were all a-flutter with flags of blue and gold, and as I steered in to the commercial harbour I wondered that *Commodore's* old paraffin engine could have brought us there. It seemed a very long way from the Thames. And not only seemed. It was.

The first sight of Sweden at close quarters impressed me in a way I had hardly expected. On the quayside of the commercial basin a number of men were lounging and chatting. All of them wore fur hats although it was midsummer, and they were dressed in folksy jackets with mother-of-pearl buttons, and breeches which stuck out at the knees. They had boots, too, and altogether looked much more picturesque than the rather English-looking Danes three miles across the water at Elsinore.

At this time my Swedish was rudimentary, limited to certain things that I had learned from a phrase-book, but I soon fell into conversation with one of the men. He spoke English fluently as it happened, and with rather a Cockney accent. He looked the boat up and down and asked the usual questions of how we had come, and how long it had taken us. I mentioned that we had left London the previous year.

"Good old London," he exclaimed. "No place like home, eh?"

I asked him if he had ever been there.

"London? Lor luvaduck, I live there," he exclaimed. "In Tooting Bec."

I wondered how this could be. I could hardly imagine a Swede who appeared to be a trapper or a countryman from the far north having his home in Tooting Bec. He saw I was puzzled, and laughed.

"You were looking at my rig, was that it? I only put that on for the concert tonight. It is regular Cossack dress."

Russians! That explained the boots and the fur hats on a midsummer's day so warm that I was almost too hot in my open shirt and shorts. I wondered if any of the choir ever escaped and asked for political asylum, but I thought it tactless to ask. My companion might be the KGB-man of the troupe, ready to shoot any members of the choir who was suspected of wavering. Instead, I politely asked how long was it since they came from Russia. "Russia? Never been there, and don't want to neither. We're Cockneys to a man in the Don Cossack choir, so far as I know. Born and bred within the sound of Bow Bells – on a quiet day, that is, and with the wind in the right direction."

So my picture of the Swedes as a fancy-dressed and fur-hatted people was quickly shaken, and Sweden appeared much more ordinary. Yet ordinary is something that Sweden most certainly was not – and not only because at that time one could not even buy a glass of beer without having the hotel manager running over the intending customer with a nose like a vacuum cleaner to detect the possible scent of a previous beer. For all the ruin wrought upon it by well-meaning socialists ignorant of history, Sweden is to me a very special place. And it has some of the most improbable and beautiful canals in the world.

The first of the waterways I discovered, apart from the canalised river Göta by which sea-going ships enter the enormous Vänner Lake, was the Dalslands Canal. I was heading for it on purpose, because in a book by Prince William of Sweden I had come upon the tantalising phrase "the narrow ribbon of the Dalslands Canal", without any further details. I had searched high and low for more information and had actually come upon an engraving of an aqueduct on the canal in de Chaillu's *The Land of the Midnight Sun*, published in 1881. But that was all, until I came upon another reference which greatly puzzled me, to the effect that there was a link between the Dalslands Canal and a Norwegian waterway, the Tiste Navigation. The reason why it worried me was purely mathematical. From the respective national tourist offices I obtained the timetables of steamers running in summer on both the Dalslands and the Tiste canals, so they were evidently in navigable order. Yet when I managed to exhume from nautical almanacks and similar publications a list of the locks on either side, together with their rises and falls, there was a discrepancy of some seventy feet in favour of the Norwegians. The Norwegian Hamlet of Otteid where the systems connected was 336 feet above sea level on Swedish information, and more than 400 in Norwegian. The lock heights confirmed the difference, but none could tell me what it meant. The Norwegian Naval Attaché in London kindly remitted the problem to his admiralty. I think he was glad to have something to do, but his government merely replied that the link was continually used and that timber rafts went from the Norwegian forests to Swedish pulp mills by way of it.

Top: Royal Swedish Air Force trumpeters open the proceedings at Strömsholm.

Bottom: Steering a Fulda raft toward the Weser.

Electric 'mule' at Saverne on the Canal de la Marne au Rhin.

So I resolved to see for myself, and by a curious chance when *Commodore* was lying at the quayside of Marstrand a young man and his wife came up to talk to me.

"If you are going across to Sweden you must take time to visit the Dalslands Canal," said the man. "It will be the most beautiful waterway you have ever seen." He took out a visiting card with the name Bo Lindqvist and wrote on it. "Give this to the canal manager at the Långbron office," he said. "That's about half way up the canal. He'll do everything to help you. He's my uncle."

With that extra incitement I wanted to set off at once to run up through the Port of Gothenburg to reach the great lake and the Dalsland Waterway, but the slow-moving geographical changes were against me. A mighty land-slide carried some houses and part of a pulp factory into the Göta River and blocked it, and I had no choice but to leave *Commodore* in Gothenburg and postpone the Dalsland venture until later in the year. But after a month or two the river was cleared and I was steering *Commodore* toward a large, square and apparently deserted warehouse which stood beside the entrance to the Dalslands Canal at Köpmannebro, half way up the western side of the Vänner Lake. It proved to be a most beautiful waterway, just as our acquaintance in Marstrand had said. We followed it up into Norway and right to the mysterious sawmill community of Otteid, where the mystery of the different heights was solved. There was indeed a difference of 70 feet in the levels of the two canal systems. The rafts of timber slid down the hillside from Norway to Sweden on trolleys on rails, a dry inclined plane.

At this time, the 1950s, there were a few local day-launches on the Dalslands Canal, but otherwise the shipping consisted of small 'puffers', miniature cargo vessels built to match the modest size of the locks, and also the fine old steamer *Storholmen* which ran throughout the hundred mile length of the waterway in the summer months. But for every ship there must have been a hundred rafts of timber, these being towed along the big lakes by tugs, pushed toward the locks by lumbermen, and washed on their way with the streaming of water from the lock paddles. The Dalslands Canal was quite unlike any other I had seen. And one could pick wild strawberries for supper every day in summer.

One day eleven years later I had a surprise. A letter arrived from Mr Lindqvist the manager, who was over seventy but still in charge of the canal, inviting me to be the company's guest at the centenary celebrations. I had only once before been to a canal celebration, and that was the re-opening of the Stratford-upon-Avon Canal, a wonderful and very English occasion involving everything and everyone within range. The Royal Corps of Signals, the Royal Artillery (for Beethoven's 1812 Overture), local Inland Waterways Association members, inmates of a midlands

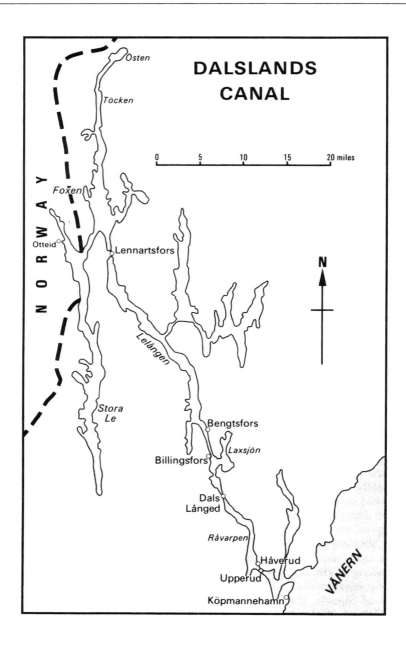

Östen

Töcken

DALSLANDS
CANAL

0   5   10   15   20 miles

NORWAY

Foxen

Otteid

Lennartsfors

N

Leländen

Stora
Le

Bengtsfors

Laxsjön
Billingsfors

Dals
Långed

Råvarpen

Håverud

Upperud

VÄNERN

Köpmannehamn

prison, week-end mudders and diggers, the Queen Mother, the City of Birmingham Orchestra, boy scouts, the fire brigade, the mayor and corporation, all of them had some part in the proceedings. The Dalslands Canal was not being re-opened, it was just celebrating its hundredth birthday, so I did not know what to expect. All I knew was that the event would be taking place at midsummer in a sparsely populated area of a country that was dearer to my heart than most others.

I have always had a very great love for Sweden. It has a character entirely of its own, and if some visitors notice little more than the sad absence of anything resembling a country pub this admitted and absurd lack is to my mind more than compensated by the sheer beauty of the country itself. Sweden may not have the grandeur of the Pyrenees or the Rockies, but it does not pretend to. Its coast lacks the Mediterranean hot sand with dry martinis under a beach umbrella, but I would not exchange that sophisticated southern seashore of Europe for the wooded islets of the Stockholm archipelago, and still less for the myriad smooth, bare, ice-planed age-old skerries of the west coast from Varberg up to Norway. Perhaps it is a matter of temperament, but to me the Mediterranean shoreline is for the most part dull, and now very often disfigured also – to say nothing of the effluvia of marinas which contain a bathing beach amid the berths for five hundred expensive craft with toilets discharging overboard and no tide to effect a daily change of water.

Sweden has a cleanness which extends to everything, but it is not that which attracts me. Poised on the edge of the Arctic, into which it extends for hundreds of miles, it has a landscape which is ancient and yet at the same time newly emerging. In Lapland – and I have walked right down that magnificent northern desert – one is in a world as free as the day it was born. No aircraft pass overhead and for a whole week one is out of sound of even the simplest internal combustion engine. The inhabitants are reindeer, lemmings, Arctic skuas, and the only sound is the ever present rushing of wildly swirling water. But the remoteness is not all. The very Swedish light that filters through the sighing boughs of the fir forests which cover so much of the land, the enchanted birches, the copper-red wooden houses with their black or white corner posts, the church standing remote in the centre of a scattered parish (for there are no real villages in Sweden), the green pastures invaded by a myriad buttercups, and water, water everywhere. And the spirits.

By that I do not mean akvavit, which I regard as the best of aperitifs with a meal of herring or anchovies, but the strange beings which seem to pervade the woodland, the lakes, and even the air. Trolls, well-disposed or evil natured, gnomes of the woodland, the strangely ethereal beings that haunt the depths of the lakes, it is not difficult even for one with a scientific training to be aware of their presence. And if any should think

I am romancing they can remember that it is not only I myself who has seen or heard them in the recesses of his imagination, for did not Magnus, son of the mighty Gustavus Wasa, become so taken with the beauty of the song of the lake spirit who rose from the moonlit water of Lake Vänner and spread out her pale arms to welcome him, that he climbed to the window sill of his castle in Vadstena and flung himself out into her embrace?

When Nils Ericson constructed the Dalslands Canal he overcame a high waterfall at Håverud by a short flight of locks which changed from one side of the stream to the other before the summit level, the canal flying over the river gorge on an aqueduct of cast iron which is one of the great engineering wonders of Sweden. In the rock face beside it is a monument to Ericson himself, and just beyond it a semicircle of clearing. It was there that two girls in Dalsland costume were holding a wreath which they were to lay below the memorial as part of the centenary event.

It was in this natural amphitheatre that the official part of the proceedings was to take place, the stately pines and pendant silver birches which flanked the open space trembling shyly as they showed the finery of their new summer leaves, and the meadow shone with the flowers of the Swedish midsummer which needed to fear no evil from selective weed-killers in this natural, unspoiled part of the world. There was a ready-made podium too, in the form of a rocky mound, and from it a speaker extolled the brilliance of Ericson and the wonders of his waterway. Then we moved down to the celebration lunch in the lockside hotel which once had been the stately mansion of the mill owners, and afterwards we all began to dance under the midsummer sun. Two fiddlers stood on a knoll under the birches and played country jigs while the Dalslanders danced and sang as happy and carefree as anyone should have been on an occasion that celebrated canal and solstice combined.

The Swedish post office had used its imagination too. When the canal was built the road communications in Dalsland were somewhat primitive, and the waterway provided much the best service from place to place. The mail at that early time was carried by steamer, and now for one day the service was re-instated. Mail was taken aboard at villages along the canal and handed over at Håverud to a mail coach which had come out of hiding to serve as it had done before.

The mail steamer (I can only call it a steamer, for that was how it was born, even if diesel now replaced wood and steam) was the loyal old *Storholmen* and she carried us on the centenary voyage through twelve locks and all the way to Bengtsfors at the head of one of the loveliest of the Dalsland Lakes, Laxsjön (Salmon Lake). There boatmen addicted to akvavit even now can sometimes see the seductive spirit of the lake floating innocently on the water. I did not see her, not even when I went up the canal myself eleven years earlier, though I was told that she exhibited her long blond, trailing hair and enough of her upper torso to make a skipper leap overboard. Then she would seize him and take him in her wet embrace to her home at a depth of twenty fathoms. The only way to make her let go her hold was to shout before submersion that one wanted to see her tail. About that appendage she was neurotic, for it was not that of a fish as it should have been. It was a horse tail.

I knew the steamer captain from my own voyage eleven years earlier, for during the weeks exploring the string of lakes along the canal I had often waited for him to pass a lock or had lain at Bengtsfors landing stage for the night, close by his mooring. I knew he was an accordionist too, and on this centenary voyage he would keep the wheel straight with his knee while he played hour after hour the country jigs and dances and love-songs of his beloved Dalsland and of the neighbouring Värmland, his singing taken up by the song group whom we were taking home to Bengtsfors.

Commodore's own trip up the Dalsland waterway and over the border into Norway was really a voyage of curiosity, and my invitation to the centenary event had come to me because I had steered up it in 1957 as the first British boat ever to pass Köpmmanebro. Or so I was told, and so I believed until a quarter of a century later, when I was looking through the catalogue of a specialist bookseller and had my interest aroused by a drawing of the locks at Lennartsfors, a long way up the canal and almost in Norway. I at once ordered the book from which the sketch was reproduced, and discovered that after canoeing the Granta and Cam whilst an undergraduate R.C. Anderson had gone on to tackle the Dalslands Canal in the year 1908. With his companion H. Lumb he set out from Christiania (now Oslo) in the two-seater canoe *Moth* to paddle all the way to Stockholm. His route also took in the Tiste Navigation in Norway. Not only that, but he wrote that both the Norwegian and the Swedish maps showed a connection in the form of a channel joining the two lakes at the point where they were closest. When he got there no sign of a canal was to be found, but logs were being discharged down a slope from one level to the other. His remarkable book *Canoeing and Camping Adventures* even had a sketch of him and his companion trundling their craft down the Otteid trolley track, and if I had seen that picture a quarter of a century earlier I would not have needed to enliven the routine work of the Norwegian naval attaché in London by asking him to solve such a knotty problem.

It is strange that none in Dalsland seemed to be aware of Anderson's very remarkable trip of 480 miles in exactly four weeks, a journey which included only six and a half miles of portages and was otherwise mainly across large and often storm-swept lakes. But they were not, and so I was credited with discovering the canal from an Englishman's point of view and thus I was invited to the junketings.

On my first voyage across Sweden I had only just left the Dalslands Canal and crossed Lake Vänner to the further shore when the nordic gods evidently decided that it was all very well for me to be convinced that the country was haunted by spirits of forest and lake but they themselves were not to be omitted. *Commodore* had reached Sjötorp and was lying for the night at the canal quay of the famous Göta waterway when the entire Swedish pantheon, heroes, demi-gods and all, determined to show me what they could do.

I was walking along a minor road through the forest after helping a motorist with a can of petrol (of which none could be obtained in Sjötorp at that time of night) when the performance began as a radiating bundle of green shafts shooting out across space from a point slightly southwest of the pole star, then there rippled across the sky great folds of heavy drapery, deep red and purple yet unearthly in hue, waving slightly as though the curtain was about to go up on a stage where the warriors would meet a violent death and then take leave of the earth on their journey to the abode of the brave in Valhalla. I stood still and watched, fascinated. No other light was visible than these weird discharges, the forests were silent except for a distant rustle caused by a deer perhaps, or maybe a troll making for cover in case Thor should fling his hammer at it, which he often liked to do. A rushing of light across the sky must certainly have been Sleipnir, Odin's amazing horse galloping with all his eight legs through the night, and as I looked up through the tops of the tall, silent pines at the astounding display of the aurora I could well understand that these lands of the north were believed to be peopled with lake-spirits, and trolls, and all kinds of half-human beings who interfered for good or evil in the affairs of mere men and women. I could understand it for I could feel it myself, and if I had met some strange being on my midnight walk back to the lock I do not think I would have been genuinely surprised. But I could well have been frightened.

* * *

When two years after the celebrations at Köpmannebro I received an invitation to the great jubilations of another Swedish canal it was for a different reason. If I had not run up the Strömsholms Canal in 1958 it would not be in existence today. This is through no special merit of mine, but it was just the way things turned out. As on the Kennet and Avon, the sight of a ship in their decaying waterway could fill people with nostalgia, but also with hope and excitement. And in the Strömsholms case the hope was eventually realised.

After passing through the Göta Canal I had wintered *Commodore* on the seaward side of Stockholm and set off in the following spring to explore the great Mälar Lake, a wonderful maze of sounds and skerries, islands and channels, which stretches for about eighty miles from Stockholm's Old Town westward. I wanted to see the island which once was the Viking capital of Birka, to voyage to Uppsala with its ancient mounds, to visit Västerås, Strängnäs, Gripsholm. The whole lake was fringed with interesting places and with history. I had the charts, but to see what happened further back on land I bought a conventional road map. This marked the two canals at the western end of the lake (the Eskilstuna Nedre and the Hjälmare) which I duly explored, but somewhat. to the west of Västerås there was another blue whiskery line marked. It was designated the Strömsholms Canal, a waterway of which I had never heard but which evidently extended through a string of lakes northward to reach a town named Smedjebacken. To discover an unknown canal marked on a road map was enough to make me head for it immediately.

So on a summer's morning *Commodore* steered between the isles of Mälaren toward the bay where the canal was supposed to start. The light breeze carried such a scent of lily of the valley that it made my eyes run. The lilac was bursting into bloom, and occasionally an osprey would rise from the craggy top branches of a dead tree to soar over a narrow sound and drop to the water to snatch out a perch. It was just the day to take a look at a new found waterway, and as I cautiously threaded the reed beds into the bay of Strömsvik I was confident that we should have a fine trip.

Round a slight bend we came to where a road and a rail bridge crossed the water at a low level. The road bridge came first and beside it stood the keeper's house. I blew off several times on the hooter, and eventually a man came out of the doorway, looked toward *Commodore* and then retired, presumably to collect his windlass handles. Minutes went by, and nothing happened. I hooted several times more, but as there was no response I drew nearer the shore and hailed a fisherman, asking him if he would be so kind as to see what had happened to the bridge-man. He readily agreed, and laying down his rod he walked along to the toll house. When he returned he called across to me that the bridge keeper could not help us. He had come out, thought he saw a boat, and had promptly swooned. The shock had been too much for him. He had recovered consciousness, I was glad to hear, but was lying down and being ministered to by his family. He sent a message that we might be able to go through the bridge, but not immediately. After a day or two maybe, or more likely next week, if he was sufficiently recovered.

I did not think this reasonable, nor did the angler. Neither did the children coming out of school, who very naturally wanted to see the bridge put in motion. Others collecting on the bank supported me, and after I had gone ashore and up to the keeper's house at the head of this army the bridge-keeper surrendered his crank handles. The bridge had obviously not been swung for years and it was a mighty construction of steel, but the road was an important one and carried considerable traffic. Remembering the bridge at Aldermaston I waited for a gap in the vehicles and got two ropes stretched over the road from side to side. Within a few minutes we had a more massive work force than on the K and A, and it also contained some powerfully built lorry drivers. We had the useful assistance of the railway signalman too. He was engineer for the railway bridge, which was maintained in excellent working order, and he crawled under the road span with a pot of grease to anoint the sensitive portions and free it from obstructions.

It would have been reasonable to expect traces of annoyance in those whose normal life was so disrupted by the arrival of *Commodore*, but an almost hilarious enthusiasm prevailed. Motorists, anglers, truck drivers and children, they heaved and pushed at the cranks until the mighty span creaked clear of its supports at either end and then began slowly to swing. The railway bridge opened smoothly, and amid shouts of jubilation we were through. A few minutes later we had turned a corner and saw ahead of us the King Carl XV Lock. It had a very grand name but it was not very easy of access, for only very small craft had been up the cut in the last years and they had been able to pass under the branches of the trees on either bank which had reached out to embrace each other and now formed here and there a leafy tunnel at the level of our deck. However, we had a couple aboard with us for the Mälar trip, and the husband had all the sense of a man who had once been a naval officer. He stood on the port quarter with a saw while I took the starboard side with the axe we kept for supplying *Commodore's* stove with firewood. Chugging slowly ahead we trimmed the whole reeded cut as we went, and refilled our sacks in the hold with firewood at the same time.

The lock was as pretty as a garden, for its beams and walls sprouted a happy flora of tansy and linaria, campanula and wild geranium in riotous profusion. There were some leaky holes in the gates which had been rudely patched with pieces of packing cases, but I had seen worse on the K and A. The doors creaked, yet they opened well enough, and when we had passed out into the Kolbäck River we could move ahead in deeper and clearer water to astonish a party of Siberian cranes which were stalking importantly in a riverside meadow. Across the fields some elegant horses were cantering aristocratically toward the former royal castle of Strömsholm, which now housed the riding school for officers.

Evening was drawing in, and I decided it was too late to tackle any more unwilling locks, so at the foot of the double riser of Västerkvarn (West Mill) I drew in for the night. And there a little crowd had already gathered. Light bulbs flashed, and a young man who jumped down to the catwalk introduced himself as the local editor at Hallstahammar of that excellent liberal newspaper, the VLT or Västmanlands Läns Tidningen. News had travelled fast from the Carl XV Lock, and I was to be very glad next morning that it had done so.

Looking back over a quarter of a century I am sure that I would not have contemplated tackling the Strömsholms Canal if I had not previously had those earlier experiences on the K and A. If anything the Swedish canal was in worse condition and it had the extra disadvantage that the long river sections were extended rapids sown with plenty of rocks, but without any buoyage – this having long since disappeared. The great advantage however was the extraordinary helpfulness of all those who came to assist us on our strange enterprise. We were foreigners, we did not know our way around the area, we were causing endless trouble – even if our adventures were to liven up the news in the local newspaper – I think the reasons for the enthusiastic reception *Commodore* received were several. First there was the mere excitement of something unusual, and to that was added the very remarkable generous and kindly nature of the Swedes in general which even twenty years of an increasingly oppressive bureaucracy and government had not been able to stamp out. But there was another cause of which I was then unaware.

If I knew nothing about the Strömsholms Canal itself before coming round the bend to the Strömsvik bridges I was naturally ignorant of the fact that it was to all intends and purpose under sentence of death. Opened as far back as 1795 it had long ago lost its commercial traffic of iron ore and even in the late 19th century the company had tried to get the government to take it over. In 1954 the company could no longer afford to keep up the maintenance, and began an approach to the Riksdag to have the Act annulled under which the canal had been built, and which of course laid certain duties upon the company.

For the year before *Commodore* arrived in the canal the total income from lock dues had sunk to a total of about twenty pounds, and this small sum was brought in only by the passage of fishing punts and other small craft in one or two limited stretches. The canal was as good as defunct, and if the Act for its abandonment had been carried through I doubt if many would even have noticed. Perhaps a few locals might have sighed, but only a very few. Most Swedes had never even heard of the canal and had no reason to be interested. But the Act was on the agenda for the coming session of the Riksdag and then, just as the minute hand was moving up to the hour of official closure, a boat had arrived at the entrance. A boat of some size, too, which had improbably come all the way from London.

Rain fell heavily next morning, and when I looked out at six o'clock the VLT was already there, the Hallstahammar branch editor being accompanied by a charming assistant who seemed to think nothing of standing

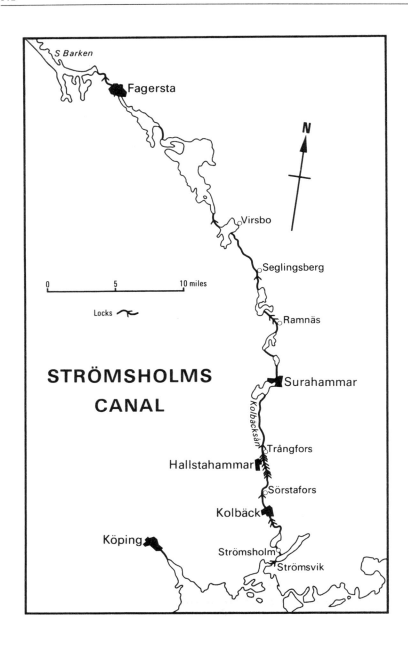

S Barken

Fagersta

N

Virsbo

Seglingsberg

0   5   10 miles

Locks

Ramnäs

STRÖMSHOLMS
CANAL

Surahammar

Kolbäcksån

Trångfors

Hallstahammar

Sörstafors

Kolbäck

Köping

Strömsholm

Strömsvik

in the downpour with the water streaming from her beautiful hair. They were most encouraging, and when it turned out that the windlasses and gate handles of the two locks had disappeared, either lost or thrown into the canal, they jumped into their car and sped away to procure some elsewhere. When we moved into the locks the trouble began, for so much rubbish had accumulated that we had to make the boat fast and try to flush out the stones and silt. Our progress was slow, but this had its advantages, for it gave time for things to get moving.

The canal was partly the responsibility of the steelworks which once had used it, and when we had passed the locks a gang of helpful men from Hallstahammar Steelworks was already getting to work to raise a lifting bridge which had not been worked for years. Later we had a canal gang assigned to us to help with the eight locks at Hallstahammar itself, all of them obstructed with rubbish and stones, and even a sizeable tree growing behind one of the gates. Two of the men were to stay with us further, Karl the iron-smith and Manfred the joiner. Both were tall, wiry, powerful, and although elderly (I believe they were about seventy) they worked throughout the day like exuberant youngsters, filled with delight that all the love and care they had put into their work on the lock-gates over the last thirty years was actually now being put at the service of a boat.

At Ålsätra Lock they left us to go home. Above this there followed a long and very tricky river section leading to Surahammar, another steel-making town, and as we rose up in the lock a young man with very blue eyes and fair hair appeared on a motor-cycle and offered to pilot us. He was Rune Dahlström, and he had read about our voyage in the VLT. He was a crane-driver, he told us. He had a small motor-boat of his own and he knew this part of the river intimately.

I was not very inclined to hand over the wheel, for *Commodore* was easy to steer if one was used to her but not otherwise. However, the young man quickly got the feel of her, and soon I was very thankful that he had volunteered. The river swirled somewhat and there were plenty of rocks to be seen under the water, and the channel was by no means always where I would have expected to find it.

Dahlström proudly stood at the wheel, watching intently the water ahead, and eventually we came out into a small lake. At the end of it was another double riser, and at its foot we were again met by the VLT but this time by Anders Erhard of the head office in Västerås who came aboard to interview me for the paper and for the radio. He was to become a life-long friend.

When the time came to set out on the return journey I was just a little apprehensive. I had tried to remember all the twists and turns Dahlström had made but I still did not relish the idea of running back down river with a stiff current behind the boat. Then, when walking through the town at lunchtime I met our young friend, looking very smart in the spotless blue overalls which he wore when sitting far above the world in his crane cabin, and he at once said that if I could wait until he knocked off at five o'clock he would like to come for the downstream voyage and stay aboard all the way to Hallstahammar. So once again we loaded his motor-cycle aboard, and off we went.

It was pleasant to relax while he steered, competently confident and at ease. I admired the courage of this young man who was prepared to take command of a boat about thirty times as large as his own, and to run her over swirling water between rocks. He never took his eyes off the river immediately ahead, until he reached the broad and deep reach above Ålsätra weir.

At the lock he politely declined to steer any further. He had never taken his own craft beyond the lock, he said. I was thankful indeed that he was not steering when, a short way below the lock and right in the channel as I thought, *Commodore* shuddered, threw up her nose, bucked, and came down with a frightening thump on a shoal of large boulders. The obstruction could scarcely have sprung up overnight, though it was just possible (this being Sweden) that it had been put there by a troll to pay me out for some imagined insult.

At once I jumped overboard to examine the situation. Even on Marken dike I had not seen the ship so far out of the water, and I doubted if she could be brought off unaided. However I was reassured by having noticed that a tug was stationed at the foot of Surahammar locks. I made towing gestures to Dahlström and indicated that it would be a good idea to get this *släpbåt* to come down in the morning and pluck us off the rocks, as after a few abortive attempts it was clear to us both that the motor was unequal to the task.

He laughed pleasantly. The tug was a museum of the canal, he said, and had long since been bereft of its motive power. I admit to being amused myself, for although there were tugs at the port of Västerås in the Mälar Lake they had too much draught to be able to steam up to where we were – a fact that saved underwriters paying for a very expensive service. Still, I did not relish the idea of waiting for the floods of the following spring, and as I knew that the hull was not holed I decided to leave the problem until the following day and lower the dinghy to ferry our young friend and his motor-cycle to the shore.

Early in the soft Swedish dawn I slipped over the side again and began the work of rolling away all the boulders that could be moved. I was still engaged in this healthy exercise when a lorry came bumping over the field bringing Karl and Manfred and a hefty foreman from Hallsta Steel. They had a good load of equipment too, hawsers and blocks and tackle, steel stakes to drive into the ground as anchors, and axes to cut down the bankside bushes. When he saw us high on the shoal old Karl wept, and he told us how half a century earlier he had watched the passenger steamer running up that reach laden with tourists.

We worked away all morning without achieving an inch of movement. It was then that the charming young lady of the VLT came to our assistance, for when I phoned the paper from the lock and said we needed a foot more of water in the river she simply replied in her gentle style "I see. It shall be done." And it was. I could not then imagine how the river level was made mysteriously to rise so that *Commodore* could raise herself elegantly from her stony couch, but I found out later that the VLT had asked for the next weir at the approach to Hallstahammar to be obstructed with boards while the Älsätra weir behind us was opened up to its fullest capacity.

Nothing could ever repay the kindness of the canal men, the crane driver, the newspaper, and all those who had worked to have *Commodore* arrive at Surahammar and then return to the Mälar Lake again. The best I could do was to write two splendid certificates for Karl and Manfred to thank them for their help, and when last I saw them they were hopping and skipping arm in arm on their way home from the last of the Hallstahammar locks, proudly waving their rolled papers in the air.

Yet a greater reward was to come than any which I could have provided. The voyage with all its difficulties and excitements had been followed day by day and lock by lock by the VLT. Public interest was aroused. People realised they had a great amenity in this forgotten canal. They were determined that it should not be closed. Help was mobilised. Money was raised by the Surahammar and Hallstahammar foundries, the Johnson Line and other industries and local authorities along the canal. Instead of pronouncing the closure the government came up with financial help. Skilled men and crafting were made available in the foundries, and when in 1970 I received the invitation to be present at the reopening there were already some 450 private craft stationed in the various little ports and harbours along the waterway.

Sweden has a way of doing things well. Nothing in the world can compare for pomp and elegance with the Nobel Prize ceremony, to which I later had the honour to be invited, and even much homelier and more local celebrations are carried out brilliantly and with imagination. It was a glorious day in mid-June when the hundred invited dignitaries and guests collected at the Kolbäck Inn to board the faithful old steamer *Almö-Lindö*, now a prisoner on the canal because in the days of run-down and neglect a fixed bridge had been built across the lock-cut near Strömsholm castle. The ship was decked out with birch saplings along the rails, and on her after deck the Surahammar town band was blowing away with gusto. Soon we were setting off down the river to the paired lock at Västerkvarn, the pair where I had spent the first night of the voyage twelve years earlier. It looked very different now. There were new gates, the walls were cleaned and pointed, and all down either side Brownies stood at salute, then threw over the ship a rain of the pretty, shy flowers of the June meadows.

And so we came to a jetty just before the new fixed bridge. We stood back to let the Lord Lieutenant of Västmanland step ashore first, to be received by the lovely young Eva Lindberg, daughter of one of the lock-keepers but now for the day Strömsholms Canal Queen. Very graceful she was too, and in attendance on her she had three Canal Princesses, as diaphanous and beautiful as girls could be.

A thousand people had come to the opening, and we sat ranged in a meadow by the canal-cut. The trumpeters of the Royal Swedish Air Force blew a magnificent fanfare and Mr Gösta Fernheden stepped up to the rostrum. He was the managing director of Surahammar Steelworks, and the chairman of the committee of the reborn Strömsholms Canal. Nearby at the top of the sloping canal bank a tall figure stood under a tree, his arms folded. He wore a strange dark jerkin and breeches of coarse serge, and his broad floppy black hat looked like that of a cardinal caught in a thunderstorm. Beside him stood another figure similarly dressed except that he had a tasselled woollen cap. This second man was holding a ram-rod. At a signal that the chairman was nearing the end of his speech the man in the woolly cap lit a piece of rope dipped in saltpetre, and as the applause for the opening speech died away he advanced and put his burning rope fuse to the touch-hole of a mighty bronze cannon mounted on a four-wheeled carriage.

The black-hatted master gunner dressed in the uniform of the reign of Gustav II Adolf ("Gustavus Adolphus" as the English called him when I was at school) was none other than Anders Franzén, and the cannon came from the *Wasa*, that pride of the King's Navy which had been overset in Stockholm's harbour and which Franzén had so persistently hunted over the years and had been instrumental in raising. (The year I ran up to Surahammar I had actually passed over the top of the as yet undiscovered *Wasa*, represented on my chart as a shoal.)

The bang from that mighty cannon sent a score of press and television cameras reeling, but it was the signal that the Strömsholms Canal with its twenty-six locks was now officially open again. It was also the signal for the Lord Lieutenant to pull a cord and unveil a monument which had been jealously guarded from the public gaze. When Anders Erhard had allowed me to peep behind the tarpaulins on the previous evening I had had to promise not to breathe a word about what was hidden behind it.

It had happened that when searching through the records of the original canal company somebody had noticed a receipt for a sum paid to a mason for cutting the inscription on a memorial stone to be set up beside Strömsholm bridge. The old bridge had long since disappeared, but none could remember ever having seen a monument, nor did it figure on old picture postcards. Local antiquarians and amateur archaeologists were called together, sworn to secrecy, and then told about the discovery. The stone had been cut and inscribed two centuries earlier and it was clearly much too large to disappear into thin air. Somewhere it must still be in existence. It was their job to find it. Presumably it would be a massive pillar of granite, not less than about eight feet in height.

The search began all over the area, and eventually one of the hunters came upon the threshold stone of a barn which looked promising. The farmer allowed it to be dug up, and when rolled over the whole of the original inscription was there, neatly incised, intact and unspoiled. The stone was taken away to have its lettering regilded, and when now the purple cloth was pulled away the original monument was seen for the first time.

Next, Canal Queen Eva Lindberg with her beautiful princesses jumped in to a speed-boat and flashed away up the reach, bearing a proclamation from King Gustav VI Adolf, sealed with the original seal of the company. At each lock she jumped out, passed the lock on foot and set off in another swift craft or by car. In this way she was able to present the proclamation for reading in every little town from one end of the waterway to the other, and when after six hours, still smiling and beautiful, Queen Eva reached the head of the waterway she did so on a trip-boat which had been operating on the terminal lake Norra Barken for just over a hundred years. She handed the proclamation to the Lord Lieutenant of Dalarna, who read it once more in a loud and clear voice to the people assembled in the harbour. Then he rolled up the scroll and presented it – to me.

It was a proud moment, and I was moved by his kindness. If I had done anything to help, it was quite by accident that my adventures twelve years earlier had just tipped the scales to save this lovely waterway from oblivion.

★ ★ ★

Of the full-sized Swedish canals two remained to be explored: the Säffle, leading from Vännern to Arvika, and the Kinda. I did not try the Säffle until 1975, and as it only had one lock (which was in considerable use) it presented no problem. But the Kinda was altogether a different matter, even if I was assured that there were no problems and that the canal was still navigable. And so in a way it was, but when on the homeward journey to Holland from the Strömsholms adventure I turned out of the eastern line of the Göta Canal in Lake Roxen and chugged up into the city of Linköping something had happened to make things difficult.

The Kinda Canal was not as old as the Strömsholms, but from its completion in 1872 it carried substantial traffic until lorries sounded the death knell of its steamboat traffic. A dear old steamer had continued to carry passengers from end to end of the canal but when the ageing *Kinda* wheezed its last some fixed bridges were put across the waterway – a foolish action which permanently debarred such ships from ever going up the waterway again. It was not these however which brought *Commodore* to a halt in the middle of the city, but a comparatively new bascule bridge of Dutch type. It lifted well enough, but whoever designed it had assumed that no sizeable boat would ever come up the river from Lake Roxen. As for the Act of Parliament which guaranteed navigation for vessels up to four metres in beam or more, the same planner either did not know of it, or perhaps was not interested. So it came about that when the bridge-man came gloomily to open his span it was possible for *Commodore* to push her head in to the gap, but not her hips. She stuck; and on the advice of Nils Nilsson, the retired skipper of the old *Kinda*, who had been assigned to us as pilot (all the buoyage having disappeared), she declined to back out.

Nilsson was a man after my own heart. He had little patience with bridges, for a new fixed road bridge at the edge of the town now excluded his beloved *Kinda* from using the canal – as a result of which the canal company took the matter to court and won compensation for loss of lock dues. He was not going to stand any nonsense from the bridge keeper, and after running off to the library to check his facts he quoted the Act of Parliament and told the man his span was much too narrow. It was not more than three metres, he said. The bridge keeper denied this and said it was four metres, as anyone could see. Nilsson replied that anyone could see it was a mere three metres, and if *Commodore* was less than three and a half how was it that she was stuck in the gap if that gap were as wide as the man said, as wide as it had to be, by decree of the Riksdag dated 1872?

The two men argued for a while. I thought Nilsson was wasting his time but he had his strategy planned. The keeper went off in a temper to find a measuring rod, which of course showed that Nilsson was right. The bridge had been illegally built to the wrong dimensions.

The bridge-man walked off in anger, leaving the span raised, ourselves stuck in it, and Linköping's pedestrians unable to use their handsome bridge at all. Nilsson went to a telephone and rang the borough surveyor, a most charming and obliging man who drove down to apologise for the bridge. More than that he regretted keeping me waiting perhaps an hour or two more, he said, but if I would back out of the bridge the problem would be solved. And it was. A gang of men arrived, chopped a metre or two off the bridge, pulled out the piles and left the structure in this unusable and partly demolished state until we had enjoyed the remainder of the waterway and returned to Linköping a few days later.

It was remarkable enough that the city should go to the expense of destroying one of its bridges just to please some foreign crank who had waterways on the brain, but of course the affair was very much in the local news, and now it was the turn of another well-known regional newspaper, the Östgöta Correspondenten, whose staff member Bengt Lundberg came down to the bridge to interview me, and later asked me to write about the canal for their Christmas number. It was fifteen years before I met him again. He was editor by then, but besides that he had strangely enough become my cousin by marriage.

That was only the first of our bridge troubles. The next came beyond the Tannefors Locks, where there was a bridge of a kind often found in Sweden, the span being mounted on wheels running on rails so that the whole thing could be moved back with a rack and pinion. To hold it in the closed position and prevent naughty boys amusing themselves there was a massive bolt at either side, secured with an equally heavy padlock. All we had to do was to unlock the bolts, wind at a big wheel, and the bridge would slide away. But there was a difficulty. The bridge keeper was the same man who had lost the fight against Nilsson over the town bridge, so – presumably to pay off his enemy – he had locked his house and gone off for the day with the keys to the bridge in his pocket.

Nilsson frowned and walked off to telephone the canal office to explain why we were being held up. He was not long absent and when he returned he looked cheerful. He made sawing motions in the air, so I fetched my stout hack-saw from the engine room. After our experiences in the K and A we always had gear enough to tackle most obstructions – although later at Hjulsbro we had to borrow a pick and shovel to excavate the rails before we could roll the bridge at all. Here we made short work of the fastenings and left the keeper to fret about it when he came back on duty.

Our trials and our return trip were duly reported by Bengt, and they immediately aroused local interest, just as the VLT had done in Västmanland. People awoke to the fact that they had a canal, an amenity of great beauty. It was nearly dead, but perhaps with energy it could be revived. So a restoration society was founded (Kindakanalens Vänner, or Friends of the Kinda Canal) and after fourteen years of energetic work the waterway was in good order and ready to be reopened. Unfortunately the invitation to this third canal celebration did not reach me in time, so I resolved that I would go and see the results for myself aboard *Commodore's* sister. So it was that in 1974, two years after the re-opening, I was again passing through the reed-beds to Nykvarn Lock, the first of fifteen on this waterway which led into the lakes of Östergötland. This time I was sitting on deck and Ingrid was steering.

Two innovations struck us almost immediately. The *Kinda*, debarred by her height from the waterway, had been replaced by another craft, the

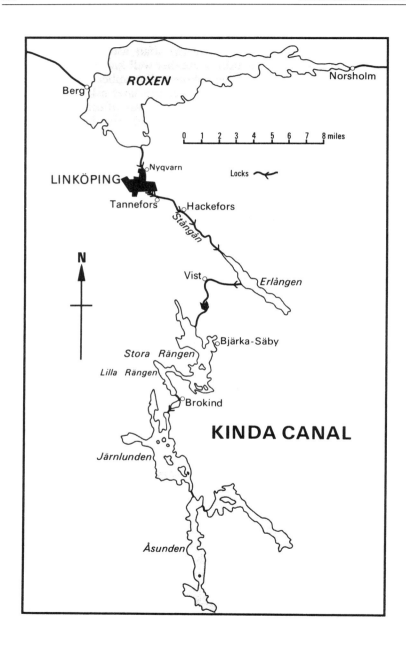

Kind, an ancient tug from Motala, born in 1907 but refitted as a capacious passenger craft complete with restaurant. Being flat as a smoothing-iron and without a funnel she could pass under the fixed bridges and run the whole thirty-eight miles to the further end of the waterway. The other change was the narrow bridge which had been taken down for our passing in 1958. It had gone, and was now replaced by a new one of the proper width.

Although I had not been able to attend the re-opening celebrations, it seemed that we were to be treated to one all of our own, one which stemmed from gratitude for the push the old *Commodore's* visit had given at a critical moment. Our reception all along the waterway was something I could not have dreamed of. Already as we were hanging in the stream below the three-step Tannefors Locks beyond the lifting bridge a man whom I took to be an office worker stopped on the bridge and called to me by name. "Thankyou for what you have done!" When I came to think of it I had really done very little except to destroy parts of two bridges. The former bridge-man seemed to have retired, but the lock keeper wrung us by the hand, and on our return his wife had made coffee ready for us, and when she came across the gates bearing the best china on a tray her hands were shaking so much with excitement that one of the cups and saucers went over into the lock. But we were not to worry, she said. The china had fallen in the middle pen of the three, so it would be easy to drain the water right out. When we had moved down a step, there were the cup and saucer, perfectly safe. Her husband slid down a rope and all ended happily.

Further up the canal at Slattefors a lady ran to her rose bush, then came to the jetty to throw the bouquet to our deck. At another lock the keeper said he would go out with a friend next day into the Baltic and catch us some *strömming*, and sure enough on our return a delicious dish of the fish was there for us, and leeks to go with it for supper. And at Hovetorp old Mr Löf, once a naval petty officer, had hauled up the Swedish flag and waited at his top lock in his best uniform, standing smartly at attention and saluting.

"Vår räddare är här!" (Our rescuer is here.) He was so overcome that now, just before the end of his life as a lock-keeper, he embraced us and wept with joy that his canal was once more in use and we had come back to see it.

I was greatly moved by this love shown to us by the people in the country; and I think Ingrid was even more deeply than I. She never knew until then that her own Sweden was so kind.

IX

Gone are the Horses

The eighty-four year old *Schiffsführer* pulled the cord above his head, the line back to the funnel tautened, and the steam siren gave a long shrill shriek which must have carried for a mile or two along the course of the Elbe. Dr Ernst Schmidt gave the order to let go fore and aft, and with hardly a sound other than the soft beating of the paddle blades against the yellowish water the *Kaiser Wilhelm*, born in the same turn-of-the-century year as her steersman, moved away slowly from the floating jetty and headed upstream, leaving the bustle of Hamburg's port behind her. Five hours later she would be due to draw in at Lauenburg, now her home port and the last place where the great river flowing down from Czecho-slovakia would be West German from shore to shore.

I was strangely moved. For one thing, the *Kaiser Wilhelm* was an old friend, for twenty-three years earlier I had admired her as I met her day after day along the eighty-five miles of the tricky course of the Upper Weser above Hamelin, where together with the *Kronprinz Wilhelm* – born 1880 – she ran a regular service for passengers. Indeed I admired her so much that I one day made my way for hours through the Weserbergland forest to Bursfelde in order to catch her and enjoy the last two and a half hours of her upstream run to Münden, and I had not long been at the village jetty when I heard from somewhere beyond the curve of woodland that same pure, powerful, musical whistle which now at Hamburg came to me as a nostalgic echo of the past.

That great waterways man L.T.C. Rolt, whose *Narrow Boat* did so much to stimulate interest in the canals of England, once told me that it sometimes worried him that all acquaintances whom he regarded as reliable in their judgment were interested most in things that were out of date. For example, young people worth anything at all would spend hours looking at early motor-cars but not give more than a nod to a new model of a Jaguar or Porsche, he said. Or they would crawl under the wings of a superannuated biplane and let the latest and largest Boeing fly overhead unnoticed. We discussed why this was so, and we came to the conclusion that in earlier machinery one could admire the ingenuity of the thing and actually see how it worked and how the technical problems had ingeniously been overcome, whereas in more modern times the works were only too often hidden away in elegant stream-lined casing, and even if parts of the works were visible at all they were – like printed circuits, for example – incomprehensible to the amateur.

Whether or not we were right in our judgment, there is no doubt that to many the lure of ancient machinery is very strong indeed. Nor is this a peculiarly English characteristic. The *Kaiser Wilhelm's* saving from the scrapyard, her preservation and restoration to be the pride of the Lauenburg Elbe-Shipping Museum and her operation at summer week-ends as a passenger ship on the Elbe, all this was due to the tireless efforts of Dr Schmidt and his band of volunteers. And it could be hard work. To stand for hours among the hissing steam and in the glow of the furnace to shovel coal all the way from Hamburg to Lauenburg – and for hours before the departure, too – was something a real enthusiast would cheerfully and proudly undertake, but the same task done professionally would nowadays be a matter for lengthy and expensive discussions with the union.

Ingrid and I had been invited to Hamburg by an old friend whom, strangely enough, we had never met. He was a waterways correspondence friend, and for years Reinhold Mertins had written me long letters about paddle-wheelers and other ancient vessels, and about obscure canals and strange locks, and he did so in equally impeccable English or German or Swedish, or all three at once. An enthusiastic supporter of the *Kaiser Wilhelm*, he had never actually voyaged with her in her Weser days as I had done, but he had read in one of my books that I had been aboard her and so he had invited us over to share this trip with himself and his wife. As we sat together on the upper deck in the afternoon sun I recognised once again the sights along the course of the Elbe which I had first seen on my own voyages along the river aboard *Thames Commodore*. That creek entering at the foot of the bank below an inn was the tideway of the little river Ilmenau which led up to Lüneburg. This mighty lock into which we soon were gliding, sharing it with a pair of swans, was Geesthacht. And when in the evening we at last reached Lauenburg the waterside bronze figure of the *Rufer* or Caller, whose job it had been to shout orders to passing ships, seemed to be hailing us as old friends. But the mere fact of travelling aboard that splendid old vessel took me back in my thoughts to that other river on which she had served out her life, and where I first had met her, and I realised that two oddities of Weser navigation which I had encountered all those years ago would now have vanished forever. These were so remarkable that I hope a reader who cares little for hydrodynamics or civil engineering may still find them intriguing memorials to the ingenuity of men in days not so very long ago who were faced with navigational problems of a particular kind.

The first of these specialities went locally by the name of *Kalter Druck*, cold pressure, and in describing this curious system of navigation I must admit that I have had several discussions with physicists about the matter and we are not always agreed as to the exact cause of the motive power which moves the cold pressure boats on the river.

The Upper Weser is more or less uncontrolled, and the rather shallow stream runs through the Weserbergland at a speed greater than that of the Rhine in its gorge. Between Hannoversch Münden and Minden there is only a single lock in 162 miles; and this one, at Hamelin (of Ratcatcher fame), was only necessary because the Abbot of Fulda had established more than a thousand years earlier a fish weir for the Friday dinner. When I forced *Commodore* day by day against the five-knot flow of this loveliest of unspoiled streams I was surprised occasionally to meet a laden barge on its way toward the lower river and Bremen, and to note that the ship had no motor and yet was moving a knot or two faster than the water of the river. It was not hard to see that these barges had steerage way and even left a wash and wake, yet they travelled in complete silence.

It was almost unknown for a yacht of any description to tackle the upper Weser, so *Commodore's* voyage was followed with friendly interest by Ludwig Thiele, the chief engineer of the river who lived beside the site of the abbatial fish weir, and one evening when sitting over a glass of wine in his garden by the lock I asked him to explain how it was that a ship with no motor could run downstream faster than the river itself.

His explanation – the one disputed by some physicists – was really very simple. With a gradient of forty centimetres in every kilometre, or 1 in 2,500, the Weser was sloping definitely toward the sea. If a ship – which had very little friction – was on a sloping surface it would naturally slide, and the fact that the water was itself moving had nothing to do with the matter. Whether that was or was not the explanation, at the time I went up the Weser the barges were towed up empty as a long string of craft behind a tug. Then they were loaded singly with potash at Hannoversch Münden and let go one at a time to make Minden in two days with no expenditure on fuel or power.

Then there was rafting. The Weser raft was a neatly built affair of trimmed pine trunks on which the lumbermen laid another six layers of timber as cargo. Some hundred or more feet in overall length, each of these specially designed rafts was provided with a crew of three men, two at the forward end who plied their sweeps to keep the raft in the channel or clear of bridge pillars, and one at the stern who worked a longer sweep for steering. In some ways the system was like the lighterage on the

Thames, but the special feature of Weser rafting was the unusual way in which the heavy mass of timber was brought to a halt.

The Weser rafts always stopped for the night. After a start from Hannoversch Münden at four o'clock in the morning the men needed a break, and in any case rafting down a swift river in darkness was too dangerous to be contemplated. The difficulty in stopping a raft which had no tug was merely that such a mass of tree trunks was a very heavy object, and with a river flowing as fast as the Weser the momentum was considerable. Of course it would be possible to have a massive anchor, drop it over the back of the raft and let it drag until the timber came to a halt, but then there would be the problem of raising it again with no machinery, quite apart from the difficulty of transporting a heavy anchor all the way back from Bremen for the next run. Much better was to have some device which was inexpensive, effective, easily handled, and which could be discarded at the end of the run down the river.

This piece of apparatus was a plough, fashioned from a suitably crooked tree stem, shaped and sharpened into a ploughshare at the thicker end and supplied just above the share with two stout pegs (or perhaps trimmed side-branches) to act as the bits to which a long rope could be attached. There were certain selected halts for rafts, such as at Bodenwerder, across the water from the manor house of the famous Baron von Münchhausen, and another at Karlshafen. At each of these places there was a meadow about a quarter of a mile long, devoid of fences, riverside seats or any other obstructions. When the raft reached the upstream end of this long grassy stretch it was worked near to the shore with the sweeps, and then one of the men would leap into the shallows, carrying over his shoulder the plough already attached to a long slack line. He quickly scrambled up the bank, set the point of the plough in the ground and waited. The rope tightened, the plough began to dig a furrow, and the ploughman ran behind it to steer it along the field.

The resistance of the sticky clay soil and the turf was a sufficient brake to slow the heavy mass of timber and bring it to a halt before the end of the meadow as the steersman manoeuvred his pole, shouting all the while to scatter any picnic families, courting couples or anglers who were unsuspectingly obstructing his course. Normally all went smoothly, for the earth was free from rocks, but if the plough struck on a large buried stone then of course the irresistible pull of the raft hurled the ploughman right over the obstacle and he had to scramble to his feet, run ahead to gain some slack, and set in the point of the ploughshare once more.

Had I been one of the companions of the former Baron von Münchhausen sitting around the log fire in his peaceful manorhouse to listen to his improbable tales, and he had told me that the peculiar erratic furrows in the field across the stream were not made during a contest for intoxicated ploughmen but by sober steersmen navigating the river I would have laughed politely and waited for him to call his faithful housekeeper to bring in the bottle of Tokay with which he invariably concluded the evening of story-telling. But that was indeed how the raftsmen worked the Weser, and if the furrows have vanished with the years they are, like narrowboats, still a memory for some.

★ ★ ★

When I travelled the Grand Union to Warwickshire the narrowboat was still relatively common, and at certain favourite overnighting points such as Braunston or the Long Buckby "Spotted Cow" one might find half a dozen pairs lying along the bank, the aroma of their cooking stoves rising smoky but appetising from the brass-ringed chimneys of the butty boats. But already it was a dying trade. Many canals were badly maintained, and although the blame for the slow death of the traditional craft of the English waterways has often been cast upon the railway companies which had bought the canals, or the civil service which ran them, the real truth is that being built so early the canals of England were too shallow, too narrow in the locks and too low under the bridges to accommodate shipping which would have any chance of competing successfully with the newcomer, the road haulier. So the nostalgic pop-pop-pop of the familiar oil-engine faded from the countryside, and except on a few waterways of larger dimensions canal-carrying in England is now no more than a memory.

This book is not a sociological treatise, so we can leave the narrowboats properly scuttled without shedding too many nostalgic tears. But certain other things have disappeared too, and my many years afloat gave me the chance to see some very curious aspects of inland navigation. I never saw the chain-ships which once clawed their way up hundreds of miles of chain to Bavaria or Czechoslovakia – or rather, I never saw them at work though I recognised the ships themselves, sadly stripped of their massive machinery and smoke-stacks and serving as harbour offices and fuelling stations in Würzburg and Aschaffenburg.

The bank-hauled boat has also disappeared. As late as 1965 one could meet around Dunkirk the coal-boats of the Paris run being hauled doggedly toward the Canal de la Colme by an unlikely pair of creatures in harness together. They had six legs between them. One was a mule, the other was the skipper's mother or mother-in-law, who lived in a poky little compartment at the bow. The mule had its own private stable amidships to which it would retire for the night, but by day the pair would plod along the towpath side by side, the heavy bluff-bowed wooden barge lumbering along behind them, steered by a huge rudder with a twelve-foot tiller. Of course this was picturesque too, but for the sake of the wiry old grandmothers I am glad the system is now extinct.

Bank-hauling was at one time almost universal in France, and the first time I crossed toward the Rhône by the Canal du Centre in 1962 there were still some mules pulling their tow-lines. They had towed the boats all their lives, and had reached a stage of competence at which it was no longer necessary to have a drover ashore or even to issue orders in the form of shouts, whistles, or a smart kick on a mulish bottom. Approaching a lock the mule would slacken its plodding so that the tow-line drooped and the boat proceeded under its own momentum with just enough velocity for it to be easily brought to a halt in the lock, which it fitted as tightly as a finger fits a glove. During the locking the mule would nibble at any grass within reach, then slowly walk ahead to tighten the tow-line and lean forward on its collar. When the gates opened and the steersman let go the mooring line the animal would take one step forward, lean, then take another, and so on until without a sound and with almost imperceptible acceleration the boat had reached its top speed of three or four miles an hour, and a regular plodding would keep it running along the canal.

On that same run across central France I came across another ingenious French arrangement. Our route crossed the Loire at Decize to a pair of locks which gave access to the lateral canal, and in former times the barges would be hauled through them by a pair of donkeys kept there for the purpose. This service had of course to be paid for, but by the nineteen-sixties the animals rarely had a boat to haul, because by then the barges using the route mostly had motors of their own. However, instead of being pensioned off to a quiet meadow of lush grass or a home for honourable and aged navigation asses the creatures were happily munching grass at the end of a lengthy tether tied to a bankside post. When *Commodore* passed the locks a canal official came up to present me with a bill. We did not have to pay for using the donkeys. Instead we were charged for not using them.

The old mule-and-grandma system was by the nineteen-fifties replaced on the more heavily used French canals by bankside traction with small electric locomotives. This efficient system of towage often provided *Commodore* and her sister with plenty of navigational problems. The normal rule was to keep to the right and meet another vessel port side to port side. But in the case of a towed boat one had naturally to pass it on the side away from the traction track, otherwise one would discover a stout steel hawser stretched across from the boat to the bank. Overtaking was a particular problem, because the steersmen of towed boats seemed to suffer from a feeling of helplessness or inferiority which led them to stick to the middle and refuse all hints that they might consider moving out of the way.

I once overtook a particularly recalcitrant towed barge by a means which was not quite dishonest but was at least unusual. The skipper moved from side to side of the canal to block every attempt I made to pass him, even though the driver of the locomotive eased off to allow me to do so, but by coming up close under his stern when he had to draw right over for a ship coming in the other direction I was able to swing out swiftly and rush past him before he had time to close the gap. Round the corner a lock came into view ahead, and drawing in below it I jumped ashore and raced up the steps to win friends and influence people by offering a few cigarettes to the keeper. He had hardly expressed his thanks when the steersman came panting in at the door, exhaling fire and brimstone. He lodged a complaint. I had overtaken him after the no-passing post on the bank, he said. Probably the fellow was right, but at least it was debatable. His electric mule had passed the post, but the ship itself had not.

The lock-keeper did not want to adjudicate on so delicate a matter, so he asked me if I had a ticket.

"A ticket? You mean a *Certificat de Capacité*? But of course."

But that was not what he wanted.

"A *Permis de Circulation?*"

It was not that either. It was a ticket he wanted, some kind of receipt.

I looked in my wallet. The only piece of paper I could find was a slip from the dry cleaners in Hampstead. I thought it might ease the situation if I smilingly laid this on the desk, which I did.

The lock-keeper took it and examined it in mute incomprehension. The writing merely consisted of "One pr. greys 7s.6." and a lot of small print about the company not being responsible if one's clothing were lost, torn to shreds, miscoloured or otherwise rendered unusable. But across the top of the slip was printed in urgent capital letters of red the single word "EXPRESS". He knew what that meant. He showed the slip to the skipper and pointed.

"You have priority, certainly," he said, turning to me. "But you have omitted to have the certificate countersigned by the Divisional Engineer."

I apologised for that omission. The barge man, pipped at the passing post or not, looked sadly resigned.

"However, I am in no hurry," I said magnanimously. "I am amusing myself. The monsieur with the *péniche* has more urgent business than I. Pray let him proceed ahead of me. I have no wish to be in the way of others."

So, amid showers of comments upon how wonderful the English were, how they came to the aid of a stricken France, and how they were gentlemen, were they not, self-denying paragons of virtue and so forth, the *péniche* proceeded ahead. Had it been a wine barge of the Canal du Midi I would certainly have been presented with a litre of crude from the cargo, as sometimes I have.

★ ★ ★

One of the longest serving horse-drawn boats was a craft the original name of which I was never able to discover. It had finally disappeared from the canal scene before I first went through the canals of northern France, but it out-lived for very many years its contemporaries. It achieved fame in May of the year 1810, shortly after the waterway link between Paris and the Scheldt was declared open with suitable pomp by the great Napoleon himself. That was the Canal de St Quentin, which was quickly to become one of the busiest canals in Europe. It still is, and as the Canal du Nord it is now a much larger waterway, capable of carrying 1250-ton Europaships between the Channel and the Seine.

The St Quentin had two tunnels. One was a mere kilometre in length but the other, the Grand Souterrain de Macquincourt, was 5,670 metres long. It was a masterpiece of drilling for its day and no doubt the engineers were very properly proud of their achievement, but there was one difficulty they had not forseen. It proved impossible to persuade the captains of barges to enter the gloomy portal at either end. The reason was that although the tunnel was straight one could not see the further end. To put in in a rather Irish way, a straight tunnel must necessarily be curved, for it has in fact to follow the curvature of the earth if the water is not all to run to the middle of its length – which is what would happen in the case of a geometrically straight tunnel.

Early nineteenth century bargemasters were not well versed in the niceties of gravitational theory and the need for all sections of a tunnel to be at right angles to a radius of the earth. They arrived at either end of the Macquincourt tunnel and refused to go any further. The engineers and administrative officials tried in vain to explain that the tunnel really had another end, only one could not actually see it, but the skippers would not believe it. Day passed after day, more ships accumulated, and a rumour began to spread that the dark passage was the entrance to hell. Worried or plain scared, some of the bargemen turned round and went back whence they had come, perhaps to find another route for their intended journey. The remainder stayed outside the tunnel ends, refusing as godfearing and honest bargees, certified no doubt as being entirely free from moral turpitude, to risk life and limb, wife and children, horse and grandma in such a foolhardy undertaking as to enter a tunnel which could not conceivably go straight through the hill as the engineers assured them.

The authorities entreated, cajoled, upbraided, exhorted and probably swore, but all to no effect. There were men enough ready and willing to take their boats through if, against all appearances, it could really be shown that the two ends of the tunnel separated by more than five kilometres were indeed connected. But that fact could not be demonstrated to their satisfaction.

At last one of the canal inspectors had an idea, and the authorities agreed to his scheme. Where reason had failed a large enough inducement might perhaps succeed, so a proclamation went out that the first ship to pass the tunnel of Macquincourt would be granted freedom from all canal dues and charges in perpetuity. This offer was also received with scepticism until at last one bargee agreed to enter the tunnel alone after leaving his wife and family ashore. No doubt they wept, sure that they would never see him again, but when his boat had disappeared into the cavern they hurried off anxiously over the top of the hill in company of the crews of all the ships waiting at the end. Arrived at the other portal they peered into the darkness and saw – nothing. No doubt there was much shaking of heads before at last a flickering light could be seen, a light which slowly drew closer until at last the heroic skipper himself came out of the mouth of the tunnel into the daylight.

The brave man received his promised reward, and he was also permitted to rename his craft *Grand Souterrain*. Years of canal carrying followed, in which the barge had enough of an advantage in its freedom from dues to be able to compete with faster and more modern craft. As the reward had been given to the ship and not to the skipper, the privilege was taken over by the son upon his father's death. Nevertheless the barge itself began to age, yet its freedom from dues was so valuable an asset that the next generation captain had her rebuilt on the same keel and carried on once more. It is said that the *Grand Souterrain* was completely reconstructed three times without losing its identity, but eventually there came a time – welcomed by every other bargemaster – when canal dues were abolished throughout France. Bereft of its one advantage the *Grand Souterrain* finally admitted defeat and probably fell to pieces on the scrap heap.

★ ★ ★

The characteristic of the twentieth century is, I suppose, the exponential increase in the rate of change where engineering and technology are concerned. It may not be surprising that the horse-hauled and traction barges have disappeared, sunk in backwaters or cut apart for scrap, but the speed with which one new type of powered vessel supplants its predecessor and then in turn becomes obsolete is astonishing. When in the nineteen-thirties I first saw the Rhine where it flowed between Baden and Alsace I was fascinated by the sight of strings of huge steered lighters laden with Ruhr coal being doggedly hauled upstream to Switzerland by mighty paddle-wheel tugs threshing and wheezing, hissing and snorting as they crept up the swiftly flowing river, the thick smoke of their brown coal billowing from funnels so tall that they had to be hauled back to pass under the few bridges which then existed. Further downstream in the gorge below Bingen – where the famous rapids of the Binger Loch have now been dynamited – the echo of their powerful steam-whistles drifted away over the castles of the former robber barons as the eight stokers heaved and sweated to shovel the tons of fuel needed to generate steam enough to battle with the great river. They were enormously impressive, those handsome tugs of the pre-war years, and I would never have dreamed that they were destined to disappear as quickly as the chain-ships had done before them.

Vanished also are their successors, the mighty four-screwed Swiss diesel tugs hauling similar tow-trains up a river now transformed by locks in its upper reaches to form an elegant concrete trough of vast dimensions, the Grand Canal d'Alsace already mentioned. And those sleek craft, the pride of inland navigation in their day, were soon to be replaced by huge pushers lashed to the end of a compact mass of blunt-ended lighters of two thousand tons apiece, bearing mountains of coal or coke. Restlessly these huge masses forge on day and night, their radar scanners sweeping the way ahead and a spare crew waiting at a lockside to leap aboard and take over for the next shift.

Of course not everyone needs to have ten thousand tons of some commodity delivered all at the same time, so the world of the far-ranging and modest family motor-barge may be secure for many years to come. But, among the larger transports, changes follow each other in seemingly endless succession, each new system making for greater efficiency in handling or economy in crew. Yet the waterways themselves have on the whole remained very much as they were a century or more ago. Certainly some have been abandoned, others enlarged or restored for their amenity value. New locks and lifts may have been added, bends cut off, tricky sections of river channel cleared by steam-chisels and dynamite, but the charm at least is indestructible. And it was that particular charm which probably led me to explore almost every waterway large or small on the free side of the Iron Curtain, starting with the placid Cam and ending as far away as the weir on the Fyris below the castle hill in Uppsala.

The attraction of waterways for myself has been built of several components. First, in younger years, there was the sheer excitement of an adventurous and often pioneering voyage into the unknown, for one could never be sure of what lay around the next bend or beyond a watershed tunnel. Never, except that whatever was there was certain to be intriguing and, even in such an industrial area as the Liege basin, genuinely beautiful, if only because of the period in which the canal or river itself had grown up. The English canal pub dating from the early eighteen hundreds, the roving bridges of the age of Louis XIV on the Canal du Midi, the splendid wooden manor-houses of the Swedish mill-owners, the bankside cranes still standing beside the Main and Moselle, all these had a utilitarian stateliness and natural elegance which often made me wish that I were a painter.

But there was more to it than just a delight in the mildly antique. On the water one moves slowly, and the beauty sinks in. So does the topography. To drive along a French country road can be pleasant indeed, but the countryside flickers swiftly past the eyes like a cinema film, and is gone. I have often driven across Europe, and if later I come to be flying over the clouds in a commercial jet and a rift fleetingly reveals a road junction or a fly-over I have no idea where it may be. But if a stretch of waterway or a country lock should pass through the gap I know at once where it is. Écluse de Fonfile, I can say to myself, or the bend below Stadbredimus, or perhaps the lifting bridge at Vännersborg, I mumble. This is not a very useful accomplishment – though once I was able to tell an air pilot exactly where he was – but it shows that a single four-knot passage through the countryside can leave an impression on the memory in considerable detail. Especially if the memory in question is one that appears to work best when inland-waterlogged.

Oddly enough, travelling the waterways opened up for me whole realms of history, of legend and romance, of which I might otherwise have remained quite unaware. Not being an engineer I could be fascinated by the locks and lifts and the huge inclined planes which transferred laden ships from one level to another, and having been trained (or some might say blinkered) as a scientist I could be overwhelmed by the afterglow of historical events which had never been forced upon me as food for forthcoming examinations and to which I came fresh and with open-eyed enthusiasm. I knew nothing of the Electors and could not have told who or what they elected until I came to moor beneath the walls of their palaces spread across Western Germany. St Birgitta was not even a name to me before I had brought *Commodore* up to the quayside at Vadstena, nor did I even realise that Kepler had been a student of Tycho Brahe at the Stjärneborg on Hven, and that his master wore a golden artificial nose to replace the original lost in a duel over a mathematical equation. My knowledge of troubadours hardly extended to Il Trovatore before I had sat on deck in the warm southern evenings in the canal basins of Beaucaire and Carcassonne.

Carcassonne – two days or more along the Canal du Midi through all those locks smilingly opened for us by keepers whom we have over the years come to know almost intimately – it was there and at Béziers that I first heard of the horrors of the campaign of extermination against the Albigensians, a slaughter extending over many years and every bit as frightful in its ruthlessness as the 'holocaust' in Germany seven centuries later, and one which even today is something more than a mere academic memory and remains an indelible blot on the past of the church.

Somebody once asked me what he would discover by voyaging through Europe. Church history, was my answer, and however unlikely it may seem that inland waterways should provide the best possible introduction to that fascinating story, the fact remains that the history of the dark and middle ages is mainly – at least in its importance – that of the tenacious struggle to bring light and liberation to the minds of men. In those far-off times overland routes were difficult or dangerous, and it was along the waterways that ideas spread through the agency of traders and shippers, and on the river banks that the towns came early to be established. At Lyon and Vienne on the Rhône one is in direct contact with the astonishing courage of martyrs only one generation removed from the apostles. At Trier on the Moselle I have been to a service in the basilica of Constantine, the first Christian Roman Emperor. And was it not by waterways that Charlemagne went to celebrate Christmas at Würzburg, and Lioba, the schoolgirl from Wimborne, travelled to the Tauber valley? It was by boat that Ansgar took Christianity to the capital of the Vikings, and even in later times the waterways were to play their part, as when the theologian Cusanus travelled from Bernkastel to the Council of Basle in the fifteeth century, and the Pilgrim Fathers in the seventeenth were towed along the same canals through which I have chugged in *Commodore* and *Thames Commodore* when the party was bound for their point of departure in the Rotterdam docks as they set out on their fateful voyage to America.

Such thoughts were passing through my mind as we stepped ashore at Lauenburg and took our leave of Dr Schmidt and the stately old ship for which he was responsible. For all enchanting voyages must come to an end somewhere, some time. More than twenty years earlier I had found it hard to part from *Commodore* at the end of many years of voyaging among the hills and valleys and meadows of eight countries, slowly chugging through a world of timeless beauty in an environment where the only sound at night might be the trickle of water through the mitre of the lock gates, the soft plop of a vole as he slid from the bank to swim across the cut, or the uninhibited song of a nightingale bringing to the bankside thicket an unsolicited concert without the prompting of a cellist or the BBC. And now I knew that the end of my voyages on *Thames Commodore* was almost within sight. She was still hale and hearty, and so were we, but at the age of seventy the business of scrambling up ladders or leaping from the lockside to the deck below would perhaps be more hazardous than once it had been.

The steersman who had so skillfully brought us up the Elbe was eighty-four, I knew, but he had the help of other hands to work the lines, haul back the funnel at the bridges and keep the boiler fired and the old engine running smoothly. Even if *Thames Commodore* was a ship of twenty-nine tons we preferred to work her ourselves, with Ingrid superintending the locking and myself running to and fro from stem to stern to keep the lines hauled tight. And now we both of us knew that it was time to put our feet firmly on land and bask in the sunshine of our gratitude for the richness of experience brought to us both by fifty years of boats, by the casual, easy acquaintanceship with lock keepers and bargemasters and water police, and through the companionship of the life-long friends we had made during those often adventurous voyages.

The Oscar Huber, last of the paddle-tugs